# THE EDUCATIONAL SIGNIFICANCE OF THE FUTURE

## Harold G. Shane

A Publication of the Phi Delta Kappa Educational Foundation

A la future:
plus qu'hier, moins que demain!

iii

# TABLE OF CONTENTS

## THE EDUCATIONAL SIGNIFICANCE
## OF THE FUTURE

### CHAPTER I
### THE NATURE OF FUTURES RESEARCH

### CHAPTER II
### THE COMING IMPACT OF THE FUTURE

## CHAPTER III
## THE FUTURE AS DISCIPLINE

## CHAPTER IV
## LEARNING DESIGNS FOR TOMORROW

# Foreword

During the late winter of 1971, I had a discussion with Sidney P. Marland, Jr., who at that time had recently been confirmed as the U.S. Commissioner of Education. In the course of our conversation, we agreed that American education had gone through a long period of strife and uncertainty. Furthermore, I think we both felt that new goals needed to be confirmed and old ones to be revalidated if our public schools were to move forward with the confidence born of a motivating sense of direction.

A few months later, I presented to the commissioner and his associates a rather complex plan for a series of three conferences intended to bring together scholars in various disciplines as well as specialists in futures studies and in policy research. It was my assumption that we could (1) reach a consensus regarding major trends likely to influence society, (2) examine their social and educational consequences, and (3) develop an important action agenda for U.S. education based on alternative futures that seemed to hold the brightest promise for children and youth in a rapidly changing society.

After extended discussions of the proposal, Marland suggested that instead of inviting ranking futurists and educationists to Washington, it might be more fruitful—and more thrifty—if I were to arrange on-site visits to the centers in which futurists were at work: RAND, The Hudson

Institute, The Institute for the Future, and various others. The commissioner's specific suggestion was that I seek answers to three questions:

(1) What is the state of the art of futures planning and futures study in policy research centers, and to what extent is the work underway relevant to U.S. public education?

    (a) What is known about futures planning as it applies to education?

    (b) What futures research and study has been done and by whom and with what results?

    (c) What techniques and methods have been developed with a bearing on educational futures planning?

(2) How can the educational community, particularly the Office of Education, make best use of policy and futures research?

(3) How can the Office of Education use, to best advantage, the two Policy Research Centers that it supported at the Stanford and Syracuse Research Institutes?

The commissioner's suggestion quickly became a decision, and I found myself engaged in a 120-day survey that enabled me to interview eighty-two specialists in many of the nation's "think tanks" and centers for probing the future. This Phi Delta Kappa monograph is an adaptation of the report delivered to the commissioner during the academic year 1972-73 as provided in Contract No. OEC-0-72-0354. All essential information from the report is included, and some short sections are lifted bodily from the original typescript. Also, some data and bibliographical material that were not available in 1972 are included.

I would like to acknowledge with appreciation the support and generosity of the Indiana University administration for reducing my teaching load during the USOE "futures" survey. Likewise, I am grateful to Stanley M. Elam and Donald W. Robinson for reviewing and sharpening the questions asked during interviews with scholars engaged in futures research. Finally, I want to thank Norman Overly who met with many of my curriculum classes during my enforced absences from the campus and Bert Mogin of the Office of Program Planning and Evaluation, for helpful service and support.

Harold G. Shane<br>
University Professor of Education<br>
Indiana University

September, 1973

CHAPTER I

# The Nature of Futures Research

### What Is Futures Research?

**What is Futures Research?** Since the sharply milled edges of freshly minted words are quickly dulled by circulation and misuse, it makes sense to begin this first chapter with a definition of the relatively little-known term "futures research." It is a new discipline concerned with sharpening the data and improving the processes on the basis of which policy decisions are made in various fields of human endeavor such as business, government, or education. The purpose of the discipline is to help policy makers choose wisely—in terms of their purposes and values—among alternative courses of action that are open to leadership at a given time.

In the process of reaching educational decisions, futures research is not limited to providing reasoned and documented advice: It is intended to sensitize the policy maker himself to possible alternative futures, to the probable consequences of a given course of action. In other words, futures research focuses on educating the policy makers with respect to desirable processes as well as on helping them to reach the goals they wish to reach or to attain the products they hope to develop.

Some scholars prefer the label "policies research" perhaps because it lacks the faint science fiction flavor of "futures research" or "futures studies." In the pages that follow, the three terms are used interchangeably, since I feel that no undesirable connotation is attached to any of the three.

**How Does Futures Research Differ from Conventional Planning?** Since man has attempted to plan for the future throughout all of recorded history, one may ask how contemporary policies research differs from conventional planning. In response to the query, specialists who were interviewed made five important distinctions:

(1) Futures planning is deliberately directed by the planner's examined values and is action-oriented. It emphasizes alternative avenues rather than linear projections and concentrates on relationships among probabilities, their cross-impact upon one another, and the possible implications of such influences.

(2) Futures planning is designed to point to more alternative courses of action than does conventional planning; to keep good ideas from being overlooked.

(3) Traditional planning has tended to be utopian, to see tomorrow merely as an improved model of the present. Futures research recognizes the need to anticipate and to plan genuinely different concepts of the future.

(4) It relies more heavily on the rational study of anticipated developments and their consequences and gives less heed to statistical analysis or projection *per se*.

(5) In futures planning, the focus is not on the reform of the past. Rather, it concentrates on the creation of a "probabilistic environment" in which alternative consequences and possibilities are given careful study before choices are made.

To sum up, the focus of futures planning is not on re-forming the past—not on refining the errors of the present—but on conceptualizing and on creating a better human and physical environment as the result of considering alternatives and their consequences before they are translated into action.

## Backgrounds of Futures Research

**Early Beginnings.** Although the deliberate study of alternative futures is a new discipline, man probably has had a lively interest in the years that lay before him since human "knowing" began. The popularity of seers and auguries in the ancient and medieval world was one manifestation of this interest, which continues not only to survive but to thrive in the syndicated astrology columns of 1973.

Voltaire (1694-1778), the French satirist, dramatist, and philosopher-historian, seems to have been the first man to have hit upon the idea of deliberately exploring alternative futures. He suggested that the term *prévoyance* be used to describe the process. Pierre-Louis Maupertius, with whom Voltaire sometimes squabbled, was another early futurist. In his *Lettres,* Maupertius wrote, "The first means that presents itself [for foreseeing the future] is to derive from the present state the most probable consequences for the future . . ."[1]

J. L. Favier (1711-84) was one of the first practicing futurists. A man widely respected for his presumed knowledge of eighteenth-century foreign policy, Favier was commissioned by Louis XV to apply his "reasoned conjectures" to alternative futures likely to face the French monarchy. This report, presented to Louis XV in 1773, was a comprehensive treatise with one major flaw: Favier failed to anticipate the French Revolution!

A century later, H. G. Wells was not only writing prescient science fiction, but anticipating with great clarity the impact that science, industry, and technology would have on the twentieth century. "Every disastrous thing that has happened in the past twenty years," he wrote, "was clearly foretold by a galaxy of writers and thinkers twenty years ago."[2]

**Recent Developments.** During the middle and later years of World War II, futures research began to become a highly specialized field of inquiry. This involved new planning techniques, including various forms of models developed in connection with amphibious operations, bombing raids, and the invention of the atomic bomb. It was in the 1950s and 1960s, however, that policies research really began to come of age. As of 1967, the creative futures research scholar, Olaf Helmer, was able to write:

> . . . a wholly new attitude toward the futures has become apparent among policy planners and others concerned with the future . . . intuitive gambles are being replaced by a systematic analysis of the opportunities the future has to offer.

This new attitude was epitomized by RAND Corporation, the dominant think tank of the 1950s. RAND specialized in providing analytical and documented futures advice to such agencies as the U.S. Air Force.

By the mid-1950s, Systems Development Corporation also had opened its doors and was beginning to provide ideas and electronic glue in the USAF cold war defense system. In 1961, Herman Kahn founded the Hudson Institute. Both centers were operated by some staff members who were either RAND Corporation spin-offs or dropouts.

To continue with our quick overview, Nicholas Rescher and Helmer devised and experimented with the Delphi Technique in the late 1950s and early 1960s. Shortly thereafter, in 1964, Helmer and Theodore J. Gordon, both then on RAND's staff, produced the RAND *Long-Range Forecasting Study,* a document that provided a kind of "calendar" for more than 130 scientific discoveries that were yet to be made. (A number of them have been realized since 1964: heart transplants, moon landings, and electrochemical mediation of behavior, to name a few.)

Beginning twenty years ago, and increasingly in the

1960s, American business studied and adapted various forms of futures research. The Bell Telephone Laboratories are credited with originating the current interpretation of the systems approach, while General Electric created TEMPO, an in-house agency for socioeconomic forecasting. Westinghouse and the major automotive corporations rapidly followed suit, adding policy research advisers to their payrolls. During the same period, business management consultants such as Booz, Allen, and Hamilton, Inc., began using PERT (Program Evaluation and Review Techniques)—a systematic method of planning and developing new products. As a new means of coping with and intervening in the future, PERT was ". . . generally credited with a major contribution in making the Polaris missile operational two years ahead of the original schedule."[3]

By 1967, futures research had become so widespread a phenomenon as to justify Max Ways' contention that methodical speculation, "the art of futurism," would be recognized by the mid-1970s as a salient American characteristic both at home and abroad. There is, by the way, great interest in futures studies overseas. England, France, Germany, and Italy have well-developed groups and teams making forays into the future. In Paris, for instance, Bertrand de Jouvenel has become an intellectual dean for futurists. The Ford Foundation has sponsored a group called the *Futuribles*, an international nucleus of social scientists for whom de Jouvenel became the first chairman. The work of the Club of Rome group, which sponsored the provocative volume, *The Limits to Growth* (1972), is a further indication of international concern over the shape of tomorrow.

As far back as 1968 in our country, signs of interest in policies research and futurism had become virtually too numerous to tabulate. As of 1972-73, the best one can do in a short report is to provide a sample of developments.

**The Current Scene.** A wide variety of persons and agencies are presently involved in policy-decision research based on futures studies. Even when we limit our sampling to individuals and centers concerned with education, these researchers range from large and relatively long-established companies such as RAND Corporation to individuals working with grants or on their own initiative. Representative of independent scholars are John R. Platt of the Mental Health Research Institute and Donald N. Michael of the Institute for Social Research, both at the University of Michigan, Ann Arbor.

Nonprofit organizations, for example, the Institute for the Future of Middletown, Conn., and Menlo Park, Calif., are to be found serving governmental and business agencies, as are profit-making consulting agencies like The Futures Group of Glastonbury, Conn. and The Hudson Institute directed by Herman Kahn and dedicated to performing "policy research in the public interest." Of substantial and increasing importance in educational futures studies are the highly productive Educational Policy Research Centers at the Stanford Research Institute and in the Syracuse University Research Corporation.

Private and public commissions such as The Carnegie Commission and the President's Commission on School Finance have considered the implications of the future, as have conventional survey groups like the Academy for Educational Development in New York headed by Alvin Eurich. Modest ventures in higher education, supported more by enthusiasm than by extensive funding, were also active during 1971-72; for example, the Program for the Study of the Future in Education at the University of Massachusetts and The Futuristics Curriculum Project at Alice Lloyd College, Pippa Passes, Ky. Another cluster of futures-oriented groups were persons and institutions with USOE contracts to which professional futurists were attached, among them The Study Commission on Undergraduate Education and the Education of Teachers at the University of Nebraska, Lincoln, for which Paul Olson was the director.

Any roster of agencies engaged in policies research that is directly involved in influencing the future of education would include business groups pioneering in the realm of educational practices. An example would be the Education Group of the Singer Company, which is carefully studying the future in relation to the market for educational materials and services. Among their ventures are more than twenty Singer Learning Centers that have been opened for three- to eight-year-old children since 1970.

Finally, some hard-to-classify persons or groups associated with futurism. Among these are author-editors such as Edward Cornish, publisher and editor of *The Futurist*, and Guy F. Streatfeild, editor of the British magazine *Futures*. A final example is the Teilhard Center for the Future of Man. Located in London, the center seeks to disseminate the views of such future-thinkers as the late Father Teilhard de Chardin, and in the process also strives to increase understanding and improve future relationships among the Old World, the New World, and the Third World.

### Trends in Futures Studies: 1960-1973

As in any other exciting field such as space medicine or holography, futures research has changed kaleidoscopically in the past dozen years. Since the mid-1960s, future studies have passed through at least four stages.

**Linear Projections.** As recently as a decade ago, much predictive analysis was based on linear projections. This technique worked very well for certain problems. For instance, if there were 5,000 two-year-olds in a community, it was easy to estimate how many children would enter five-year-old kindergarten three years hence.

Let us call linear projection Phase I of futures research. It is represented by the following model:

Model I

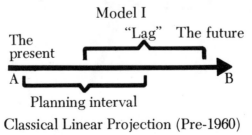

Classical Linear Projection (Pre-1960)

Model I simply portrays the idea of preparing for events anticipated in the future such as planning a new elementary school to meet a community's increases in pupil population in the one-to-four year-old range. Such linear projections usually worked out in a satisfactory manner where reliable social indicators (e.g., birth rates, production data, or death rates) were concerned. As the model indicates, one began planning in the present (A), certain decisions were made during the *planning interval,* (A-B), there was *lag* as plans were implemented and new plans developed, and finally, the plans that had been made hopefully would fit the realities of the future (B) as it became the present.

No later than 1965 or 1966, futures research theory began to change. Although linear projections were not rejected, they were recognized to have severe limitations. As a result, futures studies moved into Phase II, which is represented by the second model. Here there occurred a shift from linear projections to an exploration of *what an organization, agency, or group intended the future to be.*

**The Concept of Alternative Futures.** It was recognized that there was not a single "inevitable" future but an infinite number of *alternative* futures. And if one used *T*ime, *E*nergy, and *M*oney (TEM units) to suit his purposes, he could very often make the prophecies he deemed desirable come true.

Model II

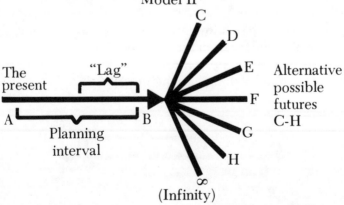

Multiple Alternative Futures Concept (*ca.* 1965)

Model II, in effect, illustrates the idea that tomorrow can be "created" or at least definitely influenced. In linear projection there is the danger that one may merely prepare supinely to accept the "inevitable." Alternate futures imply a dynamic *alteration* of tomorrow.

**The Cross-impact Concept.** Once the fan-shaped concept of tomorrow had been established, it was inevitable that Phase III would develop. A sophisticated version of Model II, the Phase III model below recognizes the interrelationships between and among disciplines that become evident as policies research is brought to bear on the problems of decision making.

Model III

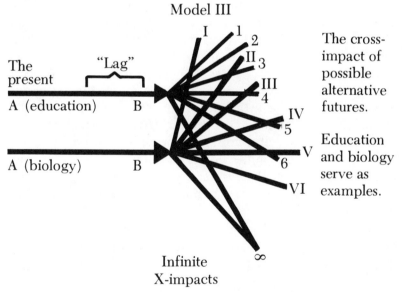

Concept of Cross-Impact Among Alternative Futures (*ca.* 1972)

Education and biology are used to illustrate the cross-impacts that the alternative futures in a given discipline have upon another. In other words, when a researcher is contemplating alternative futures ranging from one to infinity in education, one also must consider the implications occurring (in this example) in the field of biology. By the 1970s "cross-impact analyses" techniques were being used in order to show how a given biological breakthrough such as the so-called "get smart pills" might influence educational futures.

**Shall We Try to Change Tomorrow?** Phase IV in futures studies or policies research is a natural extension of the first three. Fundamentally, it involves a *philosophical* question arising from the concept of alternative, cross-impacting probabilistic futures. The question is whether or not man should seek to use his time, energy, and money (TEM units) to seek to create or shape tomorrow and, if so, how this might be done.

Man has, of course, always intervened in certain ways to shape the future. Philip of Macedon, when he developed the phalanx, forerunner of the armored division, and over-ran ancient Greece was, in a sense "changing tomorrow." The question here is more subtle. Shall mankind change the course of rivers, shall he (through the process of cloning) "xerox" human beings by making genetic copies, and shall he artificially enhance sexual pleasure by electronic stimulation of the brain? How far should he go in stimulating himself as research provides a kind of "pleasure center bonus" more powerful than the desire to eat, drink, or copulate? Patently this is potentially far more involved than, say, futures planning to control disease or population.

Insofar as I could judge in my interviews with futurists, positions with respect to intervention ran through four gradients:

(1) A hesitant "no" or a reluctant "yes."

(2) We must consider intervention, but in many instances, we do not have enough data or a suitable consensus regarding the kind of environments that are "safe" and "best."

(3) We are so close to several wide-scale catastrophes (e.g., famine and pollution crisis) that we have no alternative except to begin massive intervention-oriented research.

(4) Intervention is not only necessary but desirable,

and enough data already are in hand to provide direction.

While we are on the topic of trends and the question of intervention, it should be noted that a majority of futures and policy research specialists are becoming interested in short-term (five to ten years) rather than long-range (year 2000) conjectures. In effect, they seem to be saying, "What can we do *now* to make tomorrow better?" rather than speculating about possible developments three to ten decades hence. Related to this development, in all probability, is the point that futurists' clients are interested in their immediate problems, opportunities, and tasks to be performed, as well as in the nature of their grandchildren's world.

The increased interest in short-range change, it must be made clear, is not indicative of a long-range "biosphere be damned" attitude. No one among the persons interviewed in the present study lightly dismissed the disaster course the world may be on with respect to population, giant plans to redirect some of the world's major waterways, famine, or nuclear conflict—to name a few. All of these, presumably, mandate much greater long-range planning, and policy researchers quickly make this point.

To summarize, if linear projections (Phase I) are construed to be an early development in futures research, then Phase II in the 1960s was concerned with a shift from predictions to exploring what organizations intend the future to be (implementation of desirable prophecies). Phases III and IV as of the early 1970s seem to reflect an analytical "cross-impact" view and an increasingly interventionist approach to the future.

### Some Tools and Terms Used in Future Studies

**Techniques and Resources.** The various tools used by futurists range from machines such as the computer to mathematical procedures with imposing labels such as the cross-impact analysis mentioned above. The most important resource of the futurist, however, is *human reason-*

*ing power.* He often seeks to break away from conventional cognitive procedures and engages in "lateral reasoning," to probe "systems breaks," or to weigh "counter intuitive" possibilities.[4] One might say that the futurist endeavors to foresee the unforeseen or unexpected and to study their possibilities for improving the human condition.

Perhaps *the computer* is the most important mechanical tool of the scholar studying future alternatives. The *Delphi methodology,* important as a means of attaining a consensus or agreement among experts, became a widely used method in the middle and later 1960s. *Trend extrapolation,* too, has been used for several decades despite its limitation to linear projections.

Less widely known are three *simulation models:* (1) computer-assisted gaming, (2) mathematical models in which equations describe a particular system, and (3) three-dimensional or pencil-and-paper models that, for instance, can be used in urban planning to illustrate chemical relationships. Then there is the *scenario*—a device for conjecturing in written form about alternative futures. In their book, *The Year 2000,* Kahn and Wiener describe scenarios as "hypothetical sequences of events constructed for the purpose of focusing attention on causal process and decision points."

*Multiple correlation analysis* and *factor analysis* sometimes are used in futures research just as they are in educational research. An interesting tool for use in exploring systematically the probable interrelationships among future events is known as the *cross-impact analysis,* which is based on quadratic equations. An analogous technique is *trend-impact analysis*—the correlation and appraisal of how anticipated events will exert an influence on one another.

Yet another example of resources commonly used is the *experience compression technique.* This may be likened to an intensive workshop based on futures planning and involving key or leadership personnel from, say, business or education. Participants from such fields engage in one to two weeks of intensive study. They project, or are confronted by, probabilistic developments that might occur in education, business, or a branch of government in a year's time. As "experience compression" suggests, the person involved must reach carefully reasoned decisions and choices in a few days, decisions that normally would be spread over much longer intervals. The presumed quality of choices that are made among alternative procedures are studied and evaluated on the last day or two of the compressed experience.

On the basis of this brief introduction to futures research, let us examine some ideas that futurists have generated with respect to probabilistic developments of the next several decades.

### FOOTNOTES

[1]Bertrand de Jouvenel, *The Art of Conjecture*. New York: Basic Books, Inc., 1967, p. 15.

[2]Cited by Edgar Dale in "What Can Literature Do?" *The News Letter*, November, 1967, p. 3.

[3]Booz, Allen, and Hamilton, Inc., *New Uses and Management Implications of PERT*. New York: Booz, Allen, and Hamilton, Inc., 1964, p. 1.

[4]"System breaks" are unexpected developments influencing society; e.g., the Black Plague in the Middle Ages. "Counter intuitive" refers to findings that upset commonly held assumptions as when Mars was probed and photographed by a U.S. satellite.

**CHAPTER II**

# The Coming Impact of the Future

## Fathoming the Possible Impact of the Future

**The Four Dimensions of Tomorrow.** Most persons involved in futures studies have specialized in one or more of the four aspects of tomorrow's world: *social* futures, *technological* futures, *biological* futures, and *human* or *psyche*-futures. The four facets of tomorrow are, of course, as inseparable as the parts of a human being. We divide them into bio-, socio-, techno-, and psyche-futures only to make them more wieldy when they are studied. In terms of these arbitrary categories, what does futures research suggest that the world of tomorrow will be like?

As we examine some of the dimensions of the future, let us consider the following questions:

(1) What educational problems or issues can be forecast or predicted?
(2) Will tomorrow be better (utopian) or worse (dystopian)?
(3) What are some interesting possible developments of the next few decades?

(4) What is the educational significance of the future?

Before we consider these points, it seems important to reiterate and to emphasize that we will be speculating about what *may* rather than anticipating what *will* be. The environment about us, insofar as humans can control it, is and will continue to be what our future decisions and our subsequent actions make it. Although the analogy may seem incongruous by reason of its age, I am reminded of Ebenezer Scrooge's monologue with the mute Ghost of Christmas Yet to Come in Dickens' *A Christmas Carol.* Said Scrooge, ". . . answer me one question. Are these the shadows of the things that *Will* be, or are they the shadows of things that *May* be, only?" We are presenting here only the shadows of things that *may* occur.

Like Scrooge, who chose prudently among his alternative futures, we can do likewise unless we act unwisely or simply procrastinate until irreversible harm has been done to our environment.

Following a conference sponsored by *Réalités* magazine, the editors wrote:

> Most of the ills from which we suffer at present—the lack of school buildings and teachers, housing shortages, traffic problems, and air pollution—seem insolvable [only] because we have not taken advantage of some twenty years of forecasters capable simultaneously, by predicting the features of the world to come, of alerting us to these matters, and of making the necessary recommendations.

Let us follow this editorial advice that we listen to policy researchers but also keep in mind the limitations that these futurists themselves recognize.

### What Educational Issues or Problems are Likely to be Predictable, Projectable, and Responsive to Futures Planning?

Futures research specialists usually contend that the word "forecastable" should be substituted for "predictable." One can *forecast* from the data he has at hand, they would contend. *Prediction,* however, has a flavor of foretelling or prophecy that futurists find unpalatable. They also deplore statements made without all available data in hand to support probabilistic developments.

**Forecastable Events.** Some opinion held that the economic base of education could be forecast with reasonable accuracy, at least on a short-range basis, and that such developments as the "cool-down" on college campuses actually had been forecast. Other specialists emphasized the point that while a forthcoming problem could often be forecast, its exact *form* could not be foretold. It was also pointed out that governmental, industrial, educational, and other agencies' intentions for the future were likely to have a bearing on what actually happened. This directs attention to the self-fulfilling and self-defeating prophecy, and its importance in future studies.

Some examples of developments that have influenced education in recent years include the use of paraprofessionals, the voucher plan, performance contracts, court decisions such as the *Serrano-Priest* decision in California, and sharp cutbacks in federal spending, especially since the beginning of President Nixon's second term of office.

Without exception, futures research personnel contend that the self-fulfilling and the self-defeating prophecy were valid and important concepts. On the whole, survey participants also concurred that the self-fulfilling prophecy was a desirable phenomenon since it enhanced the likelihood that wise futures research and futures planning could actually lead to desirable interventions in the course of future events. It was frequently pointed out that what officials in the U.S. government believed was likely to come true, often *would* occur because of the power of the funds that they could deploy as instruments of policy in furthering their beliefs.

One behavioral scientist contended, by the way, that an important forecast of the moment was that schools might very well become increasingly incapable of performing their present functions. They could not assume new functions in the absence of badly needed social decisions regarding what the culture expected of its schools.

**Projectable Events.** Here most futurists limited themselves to such matter-of-fact items as enrollment studies based on demographic data, relationships between the Gross National Product and school expenditures and, at least until recently, likely trends in births and population shifts.

**Is Education Responsive to Futures Planning?** Despite the conservatism of futurists with respect to predictions, forecasts, and projections, virtually all of them agreed that much of U.S. education was or at least could be responsive to futures planning. Emphasis here was placed upon the fact that we could identify alternative educational futures and examine their pluralistic qualities, and that we could also identify their relationship to the general welfare, ascertain our ability to finance them, and vary what was offered in terms of the wishes and aspirations of most segments of a pluralistic society. The role of the federal government in shaping the future through its choices in deploying tax monies again was mentioned repeatedly. Recent economies have served to underscore the importance of this point.

### Will Tomorrow Be Better
### (Utopian) or Worse (Dystopian)?

Judging by the attitudes of persons participating in the futures-oriented study supported by the USOE, most policies research specialists have a warmly optimistic view of what tomorrow holds in store for the United States. They anticipate that humankind, through the use of collective intelligence, will manage to cope with the threats it has imposed to the biosphere and to its own humanity. The futurists' emphasis on a more or less utopian future is based, of course, upon the plausible assumption that there is still enough time to make a choice between creating a world worth living in and one made untenable by man's intransigence, his willingness to do anything except make the important concessions that the times seem to require.

Among persons who hold distinctly utopian views are W. W. Wagar, who wrote *Building the City of Man,* and Gerald Feinberg, author of *The Prometheus Project.* Wagar makes a compelling analysis of today's problems and dilemmas, although he becomes less convincing in his scenarios for reform, which suffer from a seemingly naive confidence in our ability to change rapidly the "values, inherited largely from the past, [that] are inconsistent with [human] survival."[1] Feinberg not only develops a provocative statement on goals, he suggests how possible future technical developments and their applications may help us out of some of our contemporary problems. Writers of a similar persuasion are abundant.

**A Utopian Scenario.** What kind of utopian or optimistic future do policies researchers hope we will attain? In general, they agree with John Platt, the distinguished University of Michigan biophysicist, who commented back in the '60s that the world had become too dangerous for anything short of Utopia. Here, then, are some of the hopeful views (with an occasional note of concern) expressed during the last year or two with respect to humankind's ability to make progress toward better tomorrows.

*Sociofutures.* The numbered points that follow do not invariably represent a consensus among futurists, and a few points made by only one person are included because they seemed to be of special interest or to reflect a novel insight.

(1) There will be a slow spread of alternative family structures including child sharing in the United States. By 1985 and thereafter, there will also be a growing trend to reassess "human ecology" in desirable ways with respect to motherhood, sexuality and sexual relations, a new social morality, and a reinterpretation of the role of religion.

(2) Women will continue to be a significant and growing part of the labor force, including more mothers of children of age ten and below.

(3) Permissiveness in child-rearing, which has hereto-

fore sometimes bordered on license, will be replaced by more firm (but not harsh) policies as today's youth evaluate some of the flaws in their own upbringing.

(4) Status will be less closely associated with a conspicuous array of consumer goods; there will be a reversal of the indefensible position that unlimited economic and material growth is inherently good.

(5) The world community will more and more vigorously bring social pressure for a reexamination of the so-called nuclear deterrence policies of the super-powers. General resistance to the stockpiling or the use of nuclear and biological weapons will increase.

(6) There will be an uneven but continuing decline of racism and an increase in cross-ethnic marriages.

(7) Student radicalism will continue to decline partly because the "humanist left" has not enough power to exercise major political influence. While a massive rejection of the governmental, corporate, and old liberal establishments may occur, it seems more than likely that a lower- and middle-class mass populism may lead to a synthesis of radical "New Deal" type changes in society paradoxically linked to a *conserving* of institutions and establishments that maintain the social and economic well-being of these classes. (If the Watergate scandals lead to soul-searching and to reforms that restore government credibility in the mid-1970s, a new stability may become even more likely.)

(8) With no satisfactory long-range solution to the energy crisis in sight, per capita energy consumption will taper off. This may be governmentally enforced at first, but as values are reexamined the trend may well become voluntary.

(9) Zero population growth (ZPG) will become a reality very rapidly, not only due to the recognition of the

explosive nature of the population problem but because increasing equalization of opportunities for women will decrease their interest in bearing large broods of youngsters. Barring unforeseen problems, some forecasters also argue that growing techno-industrial changes in underdeveloped countries will lead to zero population growth as early as 1990 or 1995.

(10) Although there is no consensus as to how it may be accomplished, we are on the threshold of a major social effort to attain a minimum standard of living for all humankind, which seems likely to occur in the next decade. This effort will be furthered both by the growing demands of half of the world's people who have incomes of approximately $100 each and by the fact that the other half, with an average of $2000, are in a position to offer assistance until necessary economic development occurs.

(11) With the pressure to work merely to exist removed, and with the leveling off of income, the work ethic will continue to decline, probably until some time in the 1980s. Boredom with long weekends supplemented by absenteeism should thereafter begin to result in more interest in work, including more personal home-maintenance activity stimulated by the high cost of such services as plumbing repair.

(12) Cities will inevitably spread, with new forms of public transportation an integral part of the growth. The single family unit will remain popular, but changing family life styles should stimulate an increase in high-density housing.

(13) Minority groups will continue to improve their relative status in the United States. While hard core black poverty will diminish, it will nonetheless be a severe social problem for a decade or more. Middle-class blacks will become increasingly vigorous in working to reduce crime in the "metrocore" or inner city.

(14) Promiscuity and pornography will continue to be commonplace and to be tolerated, but there will be stronger efforts to protect children and youth from premature or unwitting exposure to drugs and "porn."

(15) Cable TV will lead to improved "cultural exposure," but the continued popularity of trivia such as superficial talk shows, vintage films, and Saturday morning cartoons will continue to annoy cultural reform groups.

The reader will undoubtedly think of a number of other positive probabilistic social factors and wonder why they were not included. The reason is twofold: first, only items mentioned during the survey are included; second, many sociofutures are implicit in the techno- and biofutures which follow. Also, at best, it is difficult to sort out social futures *per se* from the other three "facets of the future."

So much for hopeful future developments in the fabric of society. Now let us turn to closely related probabilistic developments in . . .

*Technofutures.* Society in the world of the west has become so permeated by and so responsive to the applications of technology that possible utopian or positive developments have a powerful influence on possible social change. Some of the probabilistic technological developments inventoried by futures research personnel included:

(1) Major developments in high energy physics; further innovations and applications of laser beams.

(2) Continued refinements in the field of cybernetics— the realm of control processes in mechanical, biological, and electronic systems.

(3) Important changes in the quality and use of mass media including cable television, learning packages adapted to home TV, and potentially spectacular uses of holography—an evolving technique for projecting three-dimensional images through the use of lasers.

(4) Increasing success in the benign manipulation and restoration of the environment.

(5) The distinct and alarming prospect of serious and sustained power shortages and the prospect that some U.S. corporations may begin to move more of their facilities overseas to escape the problem. Such a development could further reduce the tax monies available to U.S. schools. In the long run, however, several developments could, in a utopian scenario, help to diminish the energy crisis: less extravagant consumption, more efficient transmission and use of power, a gradual shift from reliance on the automobile to more and better public transportation, attainment of ZPG, and the possible perfection of much-improved solar and atomic-nuclear energy sources. (Cf. 9 and 10 below.)

(6) Important changes in the nature of goods and materials, as in the home construction field, accompanied by a concomitant trend away from obsolescent requirements (like the spacing of studs in a house) to new, broad performance requirements (as in establishing, by testing, a structure's resistance to 150 m.p.h. winds).

(7) Increasing use of the computer and data-processing techniques; perfection of home-size computers.

(8) Introduction of super-conductors for transmission of electricity with less power loss; some years thereafter, the practical wireless transmission of power.

(9) A growing recognition that technology probably cannot provide adequate long-term substitutes for physical resources such as fuel, minerals, and breathable air. As one outcome, drastic but desirable changes in consumption and production patterns may take place before 1990, or certainly prior to 2020 A.D. Even nuclear processes (without radioactive waste) are not in themselves a complete or viable solution to the total configuration

of problems of increasing energy use and decreasing world resources.

(10) An important technological change in prospect is a return to massive public transportation accompanied by considerable decentralization of drive-in plazas and shopping mall clusters; new small chains of neighborhood shops, within walking distance, seem likely to again become part of housing developments and single family home areas.

(11) International trade and investments in industry and technology appear to be emerging as international forces for stability and peace. The corporate-technical establishment has much more to lose than to gain in an era of atomic weaponry.

*Biofutures.* Because of the unpredictability of research in progress, biofutures are difficult ones on which to obtain many speculations from futurists. Possible developments of 1975-1995 might include:

(1) Increasingly heated debate over the use of behavior modification techniques (chemical, electronic, and psychological) and over the issues of genetic manipulation.

(2) As the need for ZPG is more widely acknowledged, pressure may build up for enforced planned parenthood and selective maternity based on genetic principles.

(3) Continued experimentation with non-narcotic "cognitive releasants," which may serve to free greater human potential.

(4) Perfection of virtually infallible birth control techniques.

(5) Possible topping-off of population growth in the United States around 2000 A.D.; a similar phenomenon on a worldwide basis by 2020 A.D. These developments might be either voluntary or, as a result of declining resources and production, an involuntary dying off of the undernourished after 2020

if the more pessimistic projections of population prove valid and a world population of eight to ten billion is reached.

(6) Likely decline, possibly temporary, in life spans due to lack of foodstuffs and pollution of the environment. The low infant death rate is likely to continue, but a distinct increase in the morbidity rate (incidence of disease) during childhood may be in prospect. The head of a midwestern pediatric center recently told the writer that he already was concerned about trends since the late 1960s in his community.

(7) Increasing worldwide interdependence with respect to food supplies (e.g., consider the overseas demand for U.S. wheat since the early 1970s) for an indeterminate period.

(8) Life sciences such as biochemistry and behavioral sciences such as psychology are likely to flourish, although for at least two decades physics and engineering may lose some of their status due to the recognition that technology *per se* is a mixed blessing.

*Human Futures.* How our human or psyche-futures will surface during coming decades depends to a great extent on whether the generally optimistic future developments enumerated  above actually take place. A picture of our lives that lie ahead can, however, be painted with broad strokes.

It seems quite likely that we will begin to give more heed to the improvement of the Quality of Life (QOL) factors in the years immediately ahead—or at least no later than a decade hence. For example, research in 1971 by Dalkey and Rourke suggested that California youth (a group that often anticipates a trend) were interested in a good, but not in an extravagant, "conspicuous consumption" kind of life style. Products in many shops throughout the land reflect a new sensitivity to good craftsmanship—

even the seediest souvenir shops now feature cheap imports rather than kewpie dolls and sleazy pillows inscribed "Mother." More carefully prepared food (witness the "gourmet shelves" at supermarkets) are to be found in low economic status areas and are becoming more commonplace. One local supermarket even had on display a "frozen gourmet TV dinner"—a contradiction in terms and a concoction I lacked the courage to sample! Good TV cinema from BBC is competing vigorously with standard U.S. fare. Remember how Henry VIII, Elizabeth I, and the serialized and videotaped works of James and Balzac captured attention during the past twenty-four months.

But despite encouraging QOL developments, even an optimistic scenario suggests that our human futures will confront us with problems during the last quarter of the century. Privacy will be difficult to preserve, the gradual erosion of good land by urban sprawl will reduce pleasant, readily accessible areas for a day of sweet idleness, and the rich flavor of the myriad of cultures that make up America could be virtually lost except for a few culture pockets as the pleasant speech patterns of Texas, Vermont, or Georgia are overwhelmed by the bland, "general American" dialect of NBC or CBS.

Although in the mid-1960s—on the doubtful basis of linear projections—some futurists forecast an average American family purchasing power of $100,000 by 2000 A.D., this serendipitous outcome now seems most unlikely, as do the forecasts of a twenty-hour week and an eight-month year required to earn the hundred thousand! In the last four or five years, futurists have worked out computerized studies of alternative futures that suggest that we may need, as a nation, to begin the transition toward less leisure, more mature international sharing, fewer and smaller automobiles, dwindling resources, and the prospect of six to eight billion people on planet Earth twenty-five or thirty years hence. These and numerous similar compromises with reality are discussed at some length in the next chapter, which deals with a sample of fifteen great problems that seem almost certain to challenge us. As will become apparent, these are challenges to the breadth and depth of our humanity as well as to our future as humans.

**A Dystopian Scenario.** "Dystopia" apparently is a futurist coinage of recent origin. It is neither in my vintage 1956 *Webster's New World Dictionary* nor in my *New American Heritage Dictionary.* Since Thomas More described *Utopia* in 1516, this imaginary island has been synonymous with perfection in moral, social, and political life. Ergo, we probably are safe in using *dystopia* to suggest a chain series of messy tomorrows that are less than moral, anti-social, and lacking in political credibility. If the worst fears of futures research specialists are realized, in what sort of twenty-first century quandaries and quicksands will we be thrashing about?

As far as technofutures and biofutures are concerned, presumably we will have made all the wrong decisions and the naive misuse of technology will have hurt us badly. Let us assume that by 2000 A.D. the world's peoples will have decided to give up anything that was bad for us except what was killing us and proceeded to operate 100,000,000 automobiles in every quarter of the globe, deplete fuel reserves, riddle the earth's crust, and ruin the biosphere with further pollution. Massive engineering feats to reverse river flow will have created dangerous climatic change that is further intensified by the cumulative effect of supersonic jet exhausts in the upper atmosphere.

A variety of wildlife species will have been extinguished by exposure to pesticides and other chemical byproducts of technology, by being crowded from their habitats, by loss of their food supply, and by being hunted for their meat and fur. Fish crops, down 80 percent from contamination and ruthless harvesting, will add to a growing crisis in food supply in a world of over seven billion persons. With double the 1975 population, the world of 2000 would not only have depleted many of the planet's resources but, because of the increase in the mass of humanity, there would be only half as many resources to go around as there were in 1975 on a *per capita basis,* not allowing for what has been used up in the time between 1975 and 2000 A.D.

The improvement of harvest through the so-called green revolution in improved seeds and grains will have failed to pay off fully despite better hybridization. Small farmers will have been forced off their Asian farmlands by lack of funds to invest in corporate-type farms that could afford the investment required to use the new agricultural methods. Furthermore, food distributed at government cost among the poor and underemployed of underdeveloped regions has merely served to sustain life and increase the population—one billion passengers having been added to spaceship earth in the nine years between 1985 and 1994.

Figures cited and statements made in this "dystopian" scenario are not fabricated by the writer but drawn from conjectures and computerized projections made by futurists. The population datum cited here is from Brown's 1972 book, *World Without Borders.*

Since sociofutures and human futures are an integral part of bio- and technofutures, let us blend them in our word picture of the worst of possible tomorrows. Unemployment is rife in underdeveloped countries of 1990 or 1995. The number jobless in Latin America, which jumped from 2.9 million to 8.8 million between 1950 and 1965, continued to climb. In the late 1970s, India needed jobs for 100,000 persons *every seven days,* and in Southeast Asia and South America estimates of the unemployed ran from as high as 33 percent. Population growth since 1950, especially the unskilled labor force from rural areas, is generally accepted by demographers of the 1990s as the root of the unemployment disaster.

Because economic power begot economic power between 1960 and 1990, the gap between the poor and the rich increased. As a result of the industrial revolution, say back in 1850, the world began to be divided between these two groups. By 1970, annual incomes (per person) in the United States exceeded $4000, while India averaged $90.

By the century's end, the worldwide income pattern was the source of overwhelming unrest as per capita incomes in the developed and underdeveloped world, reach a ratio of approximately $50 to $1.

Urban populations grew by 500 percent in the three decades prior to 2000 A.D., and Calcutta was close to the 50,000,000 mark. By 1990, Lima had passed 6,000,000 and was still growing. Mexico City, one-third shantytown in 1970, was overwhelmed by its slums in the late 1980s, and plans were afoot to rebuild the capital elsewhere.

In the early 1970s, actual Atlantic crossings of all types average about 20,000 per day.

Travel—by those who could afford it—increased vastly after 1975 despite the social havoc and pollution problems it created, and despite the fact that intensive tourism became destructive of the monuments and landscapes that motivated it. By 1980, nearly 50,000 persons flew in and out of the United States *each day*, partly because the continued decline in the value of the dollar made it an attractive bargain to wealthy Asians and Europeans.

Linear projections such as these, the reader is reminded, are not necessarily pictures of reality. They merely—like the Ghost of Christmas Yet to Come—suggest what *could* happen if humankind is unwise, careless, stubborn, and exploitive of itself for the next thirty to fifty years.

Great strides were made in improving literacy after 1950 and in the five years from 1960 to 1965 the percentage of persons who could read increased from 39 percent to 43 percent. However, there actually were more illiterates because population growth exceeded educational resources in much of Africa, Asia, and Latin America. By the late 1990s, some 50 percent of humankind still had not learned to cope with print. The slow increases in literacy also was attributed, in the Third World, to the fact that during the 1980s and 1990s, over 90 percent of the world's books and 60 percent of the mail carried was written in English or other European languages.

Lest the view become too alarming or depressing, let

us pull down the curtain on our dystopian view of the abyss of the future. Let us also remember that for uncounted years to come, no *inevitable* disaster for humankind can be foreseen lurking on the road to tomorrow. Our real future can become one of many infinitely rich or distressingly barren alternatives.

### The Educational Significance of the Future

In the brief preceding examination of the future, an attempt was made to probe it in the broadest of terms. In view of the audience of educators, and persons interested in education, for whom this monograph is intended, it now becomes time to think about the *educational* implications of the next two or three decades. If, as scholars in policies research tell us, the future is malleable, if it resides in the soundness of our *data gathering*, in the wisdom of our *choices*, and in the courage of our *actions*, what is the charge that the future places before U.S. schools? That is, what are the emerging responsibilities and tasks that confront both *schooling* and the broader concept of *education* that can be provided only by the home, the community, mass media, and similar agencies? How can these agencies be used to help reverse ominous current trends during the precious few years that remain before the present generation runs the risk of doing irreversible damage to the environment? How can we avoid consequent harm both to ourselves and to the children of the 1970s and 1980s, who will inherit whatever kind of earth we leave behind?

**Education's Emerging Responsibility.** Let us begin by noting that in the late 1960s and early 1970s, it became fashionable for some writers to belittle what, if anything, schooling could accomplish. As Wilma Longstreet pointed out in a brilliant 1973 monograph *(Beyond Jencks: The Myth of Equal Schooling)*, we seemed to have moved away from the myth of 1925 or 1935 that our schools could do almost anything: compensate for weakening church-family-community influences, for instance, or improve mental health, or develop a literate population. Now we are confronted with the antimyth of the '60s and early '70s. This is the Christopher Jencksian concept that the schools actually can do very little since ". . . the character of a school's output depends largely on a single input, namely, the characteristics of the entering children."[2]

Patently, the schools *can* attain many desirable objectives. This is clearly on the record. Over a period of two centuries, they *have* accomplished a great deal within the parameters the public supported. And it is important to bear in mind—our contemporary social and environmental migraines notwithstanding—that important technological triumphs such as man in space were achieved predominantly by the products of U.S. education, as were the social improvements since 1900 that have taken ten-year-olds out of our coal mines, belatedly enfranchised women and released them from much of their chattel status, and revolutionized other concepts of human rights in two or three decades.

What schools actually can do, then, seems to lie somewhere between the myth of their infallibility and the antimyth of their impotence. Handicapped by insufficient funds, hampered by political expediency, staffed by teachers who were belittled from colonial times, beset by rapid turnover from the elementary school to the university presidency, often indifferently housed, and plagued by a strident minority of critics, the schools have nevertheless managed to improve with respect to the quality of their faculties, to serve larger and larger segments of the population, and to keep their academic accomplishments slanted upward.

The question is not *whether* U.S. schools are a great domestic resource, but *how* they can best be utilized during coming decades: how they can serve the country (and the planet!) most effectively. One of our vital tasks as educators is to join other citizens in defining both the emerging potentialities of education and of schooling and the emerging responsibilities that each can begin more fully to bear as the world seeks to heal itself of the inequality, exploitation, inhumaneness, war, and acute tensions that have demeaned humankind.

**The Four-Fold Potential Significance of Education in Tomorrow's World.** The significance of education in the future can be summarized in four points.

*First,* education is significant because it provides a tested vehicle for implementing the values of a changing society and the emerging goals to which new values point. As a mirror reflecting society, schools do not *create* the future but can mirror the culture as it changes and prepares children to participate more effectively in a continuing effort to bring about better ways of life. Furthermore, since the school population is recycled in approximately twelve years, society has a constantly freshened opportunity to redesign the experiences of the young so as to correct old errors in theory and in practice. All that is lacking to help education become genuinely effective *now* are the social decisions needed to restore a source of certainty as to the purpose of education.

*Second,* many of the basic problems of our times can be attacked through education, once a sense of purpose is rediscovered. A number of our fundamental problems, as identified through futures research, along with their educational implications, are presented and discussed in Chapter III. The basic restructuring of both schooling and education (in the light of these implications) is explored in Chapter IV.

*Third,* in view of the demands likely to be placed on it, the significance of education in the world of the 1980s is suggested by a growing flexibility and responsiveness to change and to educational alternatives. In the past, like a Vestal temple, the school has tended to preserve the ideas and traditions of yesterday, all safely packaged for the classroom. Without disregarding the past, our educational resources also can be used quickly to implement the social decisions needed to implement the best of alternative futures.

*Fourth,* the improvement of the psychological climate of

the school can achieve a new significance for education in the next decade. Security is the best preparation for an insecure future. Education needs to create an inner security as an antidote for uncertainty. The *will* to contribute to a superior, humane life style is developed in a good psychological climate. Ability to contribute becomes meaningless without the motivation to give of one's self.

In fine, education is potentially significant because: (1) It is an established means of introducing learners to emergent social decisions; (2) it can be used to attack certain social problems (3) it has shown an increasing ability to accept and to implement new alternatives; and (4) it is probably society's best means of guiding human development so that an under-the-skin security develops in each child and so that he is motivated to contribute to the culture of tomorrow.

**The Significance of the Future for Education.** Conversely, *the future has a significance for education.* The study of alternatives and options that lie ahead for humanity appear to mandate educational changes of a profound nature in certain fields of substantive content. The shape of our probabilistic futures also has persuaded many students of policies research that *major changes are needed in the traditional structure of schooling that extends from early childhood through post-secondary education,* as well as in methods and procedures that a new "educational format" demands.

Problems with a close relationship to education are examined in Chapter III, as already noted. Chapter IV develops a scenario for changes in climate and structure, in methods and materials of instruction, and in the content of certain disciplines—especially the sciences and social sciences.

## FOOTNOTES

[1]Lester R. Brown, *World Without Borders.* New York: Random House, 1972.

[2]Christopher Jencks, *Inequality: A Reassessment of the Effect of Family and Schooling in America.* New York: Basic Books, 1972.

# CHAPTER III

# The Future
# as Discipline

### The Problems and the Promise of the Future

At the beginning of the twentieth century, the people of the western world were in an optimistic frame of mind. After many remembered centuries of poverty, hunger, inhumanity, the oppressions of princes, and the tyranny of the auto-de-fé, humankind was thought to stand on the threshold of virtually a new life. So most people thought, in 1900. As *Time* magazine noted in 1950:

Horatio Alger, his rags-to-riches message in popular bloom, had died the year before. Stephen Crane, who had seen more of the rags than riches and had written *Maggie: A Girl of the Street*, was about to die at 28. Pessimism and doubt were not hard to find on January 1, 1900, but the world and the U.S. sided with Alger.

**Great Expectations.** Science, it was believed, would remake the world into a better place. The work of Koch, Lister, Reed, Pasteur, and Röntgen promised to end or to mend the ravages of disease. The abundance of the world's forests, fields, and mines was inexhaustible—or so it seemed in a mostly muscle-powered world of not many more than a billion people.

Technology held great promise. By 1903, a trans-Pacific cable was to be completed to provide round-the-globe communication and a projected trans-Panamanian canal would dramatically improve transportation. The era of muckraking was beginning to alert the United States to needed social reforms, and renewal of the Triple Alliance and the Entente Cordiale promised Europe a fancied security.

In a phrase, God was in His Heaven, despite Charles Darwin's scientism. So expansive was the American mood that Congress even bestowed citizenship on the members of five "civilized" Indian tribes—apparently unaware of the irony implicit in the fact that the five tribes were the earlier settlers. At the international level, with dedicated smugness, the Old World and the New World sent food and their scriptures to the Third World's hungry peoples as a part of their duty to help carry the white man's burden.

Undoubtedly a plurality of the 91,972,266 United States citizens tabulated in the 1910 census would have judged the biosphere about them to be a very good one—despite the fact that most of them wanted a larger share of its fruits. And it must be acknowledged, despite my gentle jibes about Indian tribes, that in certain ways it *was* a good world, or at least a well-intentioned one. However, it was "good" for reasons other than those in which most of the western world took pride and pleasure.

Here is why, in 1900 and 1910, I think there really *was* reason for humankind to find satisfaction in itself and in the spinning bit of real estate we occupied. By 1900, our species had crossed six historic watersheds and was close to the crest of a seventh.

The first watershed was reached some 50,000 years ago when *knowing* began; when we became human as we learned to use the power of the mind that distinguished us from animals. Much later, around 8000 B.C., we traversed the *agricultural* watershed that made a form of settled community living possible. This was an important step toward civilization. Then, between 600 and 500 B.C., a *religious* watershed was crossed as primitive and animistic god-beliefs began to be displaced by deeper metaphysical insights and the concept of a single God.

With the Renaissance, between 1300 and 1400, new heights of *aesthetic and ideological* innovation were reached atop the fourth watershed. The fifth watershed—the eighteenth-century *production* revolution—and the sixth, the nineteenth-century *scientific* revolution, followed in rapid, succession. By 1900, we were beginning to near the seventh crest: the *electric-electronic* era, which has profoundly influenced the present century.

What I am trying to say is that in 1900 humankind really had important reasons for feelings of pride and confidence in the perspective of changes that our species had midwifed in fifty millenia. A mindscape teeming with ideas had been created, and our mindscope was so vastly extended that in the last half of the century we have been stunned— thrown into future shock—by the results of our technological virtuosity.

**The Fruits of Tantalus.** Despite the cultural accumulations and the prodigious achievements of the first seventy-three years of the twentieth century, our tomorrows haven't worked out as many of us had hoped and expected that they would. In the United States, the first nation to begin to reach the high levels of material possession that were once naively associated with "happiness" and with "success," the impregnable certainty of our Currier and Ives morality has been shattered by the "new permissiveness" of the 1960s. Our intricate social machinery has become unstable and efforts to repair it are tangled in bickerings. Even the high-class garbage produced by our high standard of living has become a source of embarrassment and is rapidly moving from being a nuisance to becoming a threat to our landscape and coastal waters.

Recently, a Potomac Associates publication, *State of the Nation*, indicated that ". . . a majority of Americans—black and white, young and middle-aged, male and female, working class and professional—are reasonably content with their present lot. . . ." But these same people are thinking darkly about everything beyond the rim of their immediate neighborhood: declining cities, crime, inflation, and pollution.[1] We seem to be saying, "Everything sounds sensible when the politicians, preachers, and plutocrats explain it, but nothing makes sense."

In many ways, in the present century, the U.S. citizen finds himself in the sorry spot occupied by the ancient Greek, King Tantalus. To pay for his misdeeds, Tantalus was condemned by Zeus to stand in Hades, burning with thirst, in chest-deep water that receded when he bent to drink. Perpetually suffering from hunger, he had fruit dangling above his head—but it slipped beyond his reach whenever he sought to pluck it.

How have we, as well as much of the rest of the world, been maneuvered into our present Tantalus-like fix? How have we managed to put ourselves into a situation in which the better things get, the worse they become?

It is with this supremely important question that Chapter III concerns itself. *What are the major problems of our times that specialists in futures research identify as the causes and/or the results of our quandaries?* Also, and equally portentous, is the question, *what are our chances of extricating ourselves from our difficulties?* Finally, *how long do we have to escape* from what Theodore Roszak recently called our state of sick normality?

## The Genesis of Our Malaise

The confusion and uncertainty of the present, the erosive uneasiness that we feel about our economic, social, political, and moral health scarcely needs to be documented. Virtually all of us are painfully aware of the problems that lie like restless dragons just below the surface of our cities, of our worsening energy crisis, of the deteriorated value of the dollar, and the like. But what led to the mistakes that trouble us and to the malaise that is so widespread?

**The Crisis of Transition.** A distinguished commentator

on the problems and tasks with which the future confronts us, John Platt, ascribes the genesis of much of our difficulty to what he calls the "crisis of transition." During the past fifty years, but particularly in the thirty-odd years since World War II ended in dramatic tragedy at Hiroshima, there have been as many changes in our lives as had previously occurred in all of recorded history. Society—and its schools—have been severely shaken up both by the speed and the scope of events that transpired so rapidly.

As I have said elsewhere:

> Scientifically and psychologically, most men and women in 1910 were closer to ancient Rome of 73 B.C. than they were to the America of 1973 A.D. Sixty or 70 years ago horses were a main source of power, and medical knowledge was more akin to Claudius Galen's than to Christiaan Barnard's. Cooking and preserving food were laborious tasks generally left to women, a substantial meal, including pie, could be had for 12 cents, opium to ease the pangs of "female problems" was sold over the counter and through Sears, Roebuck catalog, and children of 8 and 10 worked 12-hour days in the coal mines. Furthermore, these youngsters were expected to be seen rather than heard at the evening meal that brought the family together from a variety of tasks, many of which are unknown in the present generation.

> At the risk of digression, note that much of the importance of the great transition that was to follow between 1920 and the present resided in a whole series of inventions such as the refrigerator, which, in freeing women from the drudgery of the kitchen, set the stage for an upheaval in the way the family of 1910 lived. Today approximately 40 per cent of the mothers of young children in the United States work full-time *outside* the home. As William H. Kilpatrick foresaw with remarkable prescience in 1926, children now learn neither extensively nor exclusively from their parents—both of whom are away for many hours in a mysterious place "out there." Although our developmental data are incomplete, this lack of contact may well account for a host of ills in the child and in the adolescent he becomes: disorientation, identity crises, lack of

understanding of how goods are produced, a love-deficit that leads to faulty intrafamily relationships, and the comparable problems with major implications for both school and society.[2]

The time-line below suggests a very few of the social, technological, biological, and human changes that erupted so rapidly after 1940 that *change itself* became one of the few stable elements in a whirling dervish environment. Indeed, we have come to expect changes and to take them for granted. While we cannot rank in order of importance the significance of the events symbolized in the sample in Figure 1, probably our children and youth have been, and will continue to be, most profoundly influenced by the speed and ease of worldwide travel, growing levels of aspiration throughout the globe, widespread television, and new developments and problems in our energy sources.

**Figure 1:**
**Dramatic Developments: 1940 to Date**

| 1940 | 1950 | 1960 | 1970 | 1980 |
|------|------|------|------|------|
| radar | dimming U.S. image | | artificial life | |
| jet aircraft | sputnik | social unrest | energy crisis manned satellites | |
| atomic nuclear power | pandemic TV | dissent | Moon landings | |
| | supersonic speed | Venus probe | possible ecocatastrophe holography | |
| | growing aspirations | | Martian photographs | |
| | | organ transplants | | |
| continuing inflation | | | lasers | |

To put it simply, change has confronted us so rapidly that we have been wrenched from *yesterday* and thrust into *tomorrow* without having been given an opportunity to adjust ourselves to *today.* As Alvin Toffler phrased it years before he published *Future Shock,* we are suffering from ". . . the dizzying disorientation brought on by the premature arrival of the future."[3]

This phenomenon of *future* shock is analogous to *culture* shock. As travelers to Latin America, Asia, Africa, and elsewhere have noted, culture shock is an often violent, psychosomatic reaction that results when one is submerged in a new and oftentimes incomprehensible way of life; a life markedly different from the one with which he was familiar. He may find, as Edward T. Hall has pointed out, how different are the concepts of territoriality, privacy, space, time, or status from one culture to another.

In effect, the crisis of transition has subjected us to new customs, changed behaviors, and strange mores and morals *in our own land and in our own time.* The transition has left us feeling alien—as if we were in a different land—with one big difference! We never left home! Nor is there any place to which we can return. We had thrust upon us a new way of life, a novel culture, which to our astonishment was ours, but transformed and unfamiliar. Small wonder that our life and the times have sometimes failed to make sense to us.

**The Crisis of Saturation.** Platt's concept of the transition crisis has been extended by Dennis Gabor, the father of the science of holography, who won the Nobel Prize for physics in 1971, and who also was, some ten or fifteen years ago, among the earliest pioneers to explore the future as a field of inquiry. Gabor pointed out in *The Mature Society* that *growth addiction* has become a universal creed that recognizes no ideological frontiers. "*Growth,*" he wrote, "*has become synonymous with hope.*" Not only has technological growth exploded during the crisis of transition, Gabor seems to tell us, we are also hooked on it.

> Under the day-to-day pressure of business, even highly intelligent people refused to think of the long term, and if they thought about it at all, they unconsciously repeated St. Augustine's prayer: "Lord, make me good, but not yet!" Let exponential growth continue in my time.[4]

Gabor concludes that the present crisis is a crisis of

*saturation* of the sort foreseen forty or more years ago by J. M. Keynes, but rejected until recently by many economists. Our saturation and dissatisfaction with consumer goods has resulted in vacant minds and in danger to the biosphere, he argues. Quality, not material consumption, must now become our goal.

The genesis of our malaise in the 1970s, then, seems to be twofold. (1) We have been exposed to too much change with too little time to adjust or adapt ourselves to its rapid tempo, and (2) we have (at least in the West) become saturated with and then sated with *things* without attaining either satisfaction or fulfillment.

### An Inventory of the Major Problems in Which Our Age Specializes

**The Crisis of Crises.** Some while back, during the mid-1960s, the crisis of transition and its closely linked Siamese twin, the crisis of saturation, took a turn for the worse. Crisis followed crisis as campus unrest exploded, ghettos burned, protest groups marched, the U.S. image grew tarnished overseas, and the nation, threatened by the war in Southeast Asia and a dozen similar centrifugal forces, seemed ready to fly apart.

Let us attempt to prove this compounding of crises by looking at ten of its important components as identified by mathematics, demographers, logicians, natural and physical scientists, systems analysts, and other persons with comparable or analagous backgrounds, who are employed in futures research centers. Let us begin by listing our catastrophes—by drawing a profile of our problems. Here is the roster:

( 1)  The value crisis
( 2)  Disagreement as to the "good life"
( 3)  The credibility gap
( 4)  Institutional overload
( 5)  Equity versus equality
( 6)  The tacit rejection of democracy
( 7)  Lack of a future-focused role image (FFRI) for youth

( 8) Insensitivity to changing patterns of survival behavior
( 9) Naive use of technology and consequent ecological problems
(10) The have and have-not problem

Let us take up in turn each of the components of our crisis of crises and, like pieces of a mosaic, fit them together to see what sort of picture of our problems takes form.

**The Value Crisis: What Do We Believe In?** Most persons in their forties or older grew up in an America that seemed stable and secure with respect to what was "right" and "good." This was especially true of "Middle America," which probably constituted an even broader segment of the population in 1920 than it does today. The nature of the amenities and the social proprieties was clearly understood. One was brought up "knowing" the answer as to what was good taste, proper dress, and appropriate social behavior. Let me illustrate with a personal example.

As a youngster of primary school age in the 1920s, I was returning from San Francisco to Chicago with my parents. Also aboard the train were two young women—the "liberated flappers" of the day. After eating in the dining car, these ladies would make their way down the swaying aisles of the sleeper and the coaches to the observation car which had an open rear platform. Here they would smoke a cigarette or two.

Let me say that the "proper ladies" aboard—my thirty-two-year-old mother among them—were scandalized by the smokers! Representing the consensus of respectability on the train, I can remember Mother saying, "A woman who will smoke will drink—and a woman who will drink will do other things." I knew about smoking and drinking, but I was fascinated at the age of five or six by the "other things" because my parents were so utterly vague when I asked about them.

My fragment of the remembered past reflects the moral

imperialism of yesterday's absolute values. Today we have a value crisis because the certainties have been swept away. We are uncertain and indecisive with respect to such matters as drug abuse, the sale of pornography, the role of women, sexual mores, the emerging functions that the churches might perform, the publicized decline of the work ethic, and so on.

**Disagreement as to the Good Life: A Conceptual Crisis.** A lack of agreement as to the nature of the "best" way of life and what constitutes the Good Society has in itself generated a crisis. Deep cleavages that occurred in the 1960s have carried over to the 1970s with respect to the question of what are desirable ways of life. What is the life style we seek, and what does it imply for social, economic, and political policies? What practices need to be accepted as we seek to cope with ethnic, ecological, industrial, religious, and business-labor problems?

The schools, a brightly polished speculum reflecting society, are deeply troubled because of the murky images they are obliged to mirror. They are experiencing a serious problem in identifying the nature of the educated contemporary man and woman when there is an absence of clear social agreement as to the life to which the schools traditionally have been expected to help them to contribute.

**The Credibility Gap: What Can One Believe?** The loss of credibility—of *Glaubwürdigkeit*—by persons and groups in authority and positions of responsibility is creating yet another American dilemma. Industry, social institutions, the military, and our government—all have felt the force of the erosion of confidence. Perhaps the worst blows to governmental credibility were the Watergate revelations coming on top of a string of earlier misrepresentations: U-2 spy flights over Russia, the Bay of Pigs fiasco, and deliberate disguising of the U.S. involvement and tactics in Southeast Asia. Industry, too, has suffered, as when Detroit insisted that antipollution devices could not be devised to meet new standards by 1975 or 1976—and some foreign car manufacturers managed to meet them satisfactorily in 1972 and

1973. Other examples are equally easy to find.

A concomitant of the worsening credibility crisis has been the way in which legally and morally constituted authorities—parents, teachers, the pulpit, law enforcement agencies, courts, Congress, and the President—have had their authority questioned, ignored, and threatened.

**Institutional Overload: Can Social Structures Do Their Jobs?** Many of the critical difficulties that have arisen to plague us (especially derisive and ambivalent attitudes toward authority) have contributed to the problem of institutional overload: the growing inability of institutions such as our schools and the courts of law to adjust and to adapt themselves to new tasks that have been thrust upon them. In part, this situation may be attributed to the fact that some agencies, such as the schools, have been called on repeatedly to assume responsibilities that they simply were not designed to fill and that they are at present neither prepared nor funded to handle. Bureaucracy has compounded the problem and has helped to keep at least some of our institutions from carrying out their wonted functions.

**Equity as Opposed to Equality: Do We Really Respect "Egalité"?** The matter of what constitutes "equity" has become a problem according to futurists. How, for instance, does an *equitable* education or job opportunity differ (if it does differ) from a merely equal one? Is merely equal treatment fair and just, or does justice reside in *different* treatment for the gifted, the disadvantaged, the culturally different, the handicapped, the very young, or the elderly. Does special provision for special clusters of people discriminate against the persons who do *not* receive special attention and for whom there is relatively less to spend for education or job training? Are they disadvantaged by being "average" or "normal?"

**The Tacit Rejection of Democracy: Do We Really Seek Equality?** A subtle point, one closely linked to the equity quandary, is the unrecognized rejection of democracy both in the United States and elsewhere in many of the developed nations. Judging by overt *behavior* rather than by what citizens *say*, a large majority does not seek an egalitarian society. Rather they seek *equality with the top 10 percent of the population.* A merely proportionately equal share of the material goods and privileges provided by a technologically sophisticated society is not especially appealing. Rather, democracy is conceived of as an institution for facilitating upward mobility, as a means of rising above one's father's station in life. Unfortunately, neither democracy nor U.S. education has an adequate coping doctrine with which to confront the inevitable resentment of young adults who become psychologically corroded by frustration as they begin to realize that they have failed to find room at the top and as a consequence are dissatisfied as production workers, sales personnel, technicians, and so on.

**Lack of a Future-focused Role Image (FFRI) for Youth: Is Life Worth a Real Effort?** A projection of the preceding point leads us to yet another cul-de-sac in the culture—the result of our failure to help children and youth develop a personally, socially, and vocationally satisfying self image that will prove to be realistic as they grow older. The lack of a viable future-focused role image poses a task of considerable consequence to our schools as they endeavor to motivate more young learners to conceive of themselves in tomorrow's world of work—a future in which they experience dignity, respect, and other rewards in any one of many socially useful jobs rather than wistfully longing for one of the so-called prestige jobs, which require and employ only a small fraction of our manpower as professional workers, executives, owners, and entrepreneurs.

**Insensitivity to Changing Survival Behavior Patterns: Will the Drive to Dominate Destroy Us?** In the almost continuous eras of scarcity that preceded the development of industrial capacities in the western world, successful survival behavior often involved becoming a part of the hereditary, ecclestical, and military minorities that had their pick of the simple luxuries that were available. Today, with a substantial array of consumer goods and services available to most Americans, we have the problem of changing our patterns of survival behavior from medieval attitudes of suspicion, self-aggrandizement, and competition for scarce goods. Our survival as human beings (and perhaps even as a species) today depends to an increasing degree on mutual understanding, empathy, ability to reach agreement through interaction and reasonable compromise rather than by resort to force or by "pulling rank." Obsolete ideas regarding roads to survival need to be discarded quickly so that schools will be in a better position to free children and youth to develop more ecologically sound and humane relationships.

Lester Brown phrased this problem very well in *World Without Borders* when he noted that:

Not only are many of man's institutions incapable of resolving the problem he now faces, but his values, inherited from the past, are inconsistent with his survival. Values which are widely held . . . are becoming threats to our future well-being. Man must evolve a new social ethic. . . .

**Naive Use of Technology: Can We Keep Our Machines from Running Us?** For approximately a quarter of a century, and beginning most conspicuously in the United States, naive use has been made of technology to a point at which many ecologists and other scientists are deeply concerned lest—within the span of the next generation—irreparable damage be done to the environment. The technogenic stigmata created by the "growth" and "exploitation" phenomena of the recent past can be observed nearly everywhere. They include the energy crisis, dwindling arable lands, the increase in emphysema, lung cancer, and mercury, lead, and cadmium poisoning. Since 1900, one species of animal has become extinct each year; over seventy since the century's beginning. Perhaps most ominous is the prospect that the world's climates will be adversely affected in the near future by atmospheric pollution.

Just as *misuse* has created many present difficulties, so the *wise* use of technological developments is needed to extricate us from the pitfalls in which we find ourselves. In the process we must be wary that we do not demonize technology. The fault is not in our skills but in ourselves, and we need to find technically sound procedures to overcome technogenic crises.

Ward and Dubos state the situation most deftly in *Only One Earth: The Care and Maintenance of a Small Planet:*

> There is a profound paradox in the fact that four centuries of intense scientific work focused on the dissection of the seamless web of existence and resulting in ever more precise but highly specialized human knowledge, has led to a new and unexpected vision of the unity, continuity, and interdependence of the entire cosmos.[5]

We need to approach the more prudent use of technology with this vision in mind and seek to restore the integrity of our cosmos. One of the most dramatic and promising signs that we are facing up to our technochallenges is the Report of the National Commission on Resources Policy which made its recommendations to Congress and the White House in the late spring of 1973. Among the recommendations: improved use of our resources, tougher conservation and environmental protection policies, technological and research priorities, waste management including recycling, the use of penalties and incentives, other environmental preservation techniques, and public education designed to reshape values. A striking commission suggestion: that virgin materials be taxed at the time they are subtracted from our resources, this tax to be rebated when recycled resources are turned in at a designated repository.

**The Haves and the Have-nots: Is There a Way to End the Maldistribution of Wealth?** A strong case can be made that the gap between the rich and the poor is the most explosively dangerous of the woes that many futures researchers call to our attention. Buckminster Fuller points out that half of the world's people have an annual income approximating $2000 while the remainder averages less than $100. Ward and Dubos make the point that in a sixty-eight-year lifetime an American child ". . . is going to run through the biosphere's available supplies at least 500 times faster than an Indian baby. . . ." For his part, Brown calls to our attention that not only is the rich-poor gap a great chasm, but it is increasing. If one projects 1970 trends, when United States-Indian incomes in dollars had a ratio of about forty to one, the ratio could reach fifty to one by the year 2000 (although population rates could of course change the linear calculus).

As a further pessimistic note, not only are our resources for both the haves and the have-nots diminishing—rapid population increases since 1950 have further taxed the biosphere. There are now five people aboard spaceship earth for every four humans in 1950. On a per capita basis, then, *even if no resources had been used,* there was a 20 percent decrease in the goods and in the resources to be shared among the more than three billion souls aboard in 1970.

The genesis of the have and the have-not crisis resides in three components: unwise use of technology, rapid increases in world population, and consequential ecological problems. What it boils down to is this. In the early 1970s, the United States with approximately 6 percent of the world population, was consuming two-thirds of the raw materials such as copper, coal, and oil that comprise the world's GNP. Theoretically, in 1973, if we increased our consumption by 50 percent, we could absorb all of the world's consumer goods. Even now the purchasing power of Americans at the U.S. poverty level is about 1000% higher than the consumption level of one and one-half billion human beings in so-called developing countries. As one result, the world's "have" nations—especially the United States—are on a collision course with the impoverished Third World and are severely harming the ecosphere in the process. It seems clear, in terms of the welfare of the planet, that we must recognize the limits to affluence, to technological exploitation, and to population increase, and endeavor to move toward a policy that will reconcile people everywhere to the need to find satisfaction from sources other than acquiring material possessions. Marcus Aurelius, in his *Meditations*, put it very well when he said, "What is not good for the swarm is not good for the bee."

For the most part, these ten problems and the ineffably complex dilemmas and issues they pose have not been thoroughly attacked or even widely discussed either by education or by the general population. Not unexpectedly in this circumstance, no serious thought has been given to their implications for curriculum change.

As implied at the outset of this section, one of the pressing responsibilities of leadership in education is to begin to find ways in which social decisions can be reached on problems like those above. Fortunately, the mid-1970s can be a time of brightening prospects for making these deferred decisions, a time in which to design the instructional strategies toward which they can help the schools to move.

### Will We Make It? Hopeful Prospects for Achieving Significant Socio-educational Changes: 1973-1985

At first reading, the futurists' problem-and-crisis inventory encapsulated in the ten points above is likely to seem overwhelming. If most of these dilemmas were created over a fifty-year interval (1920 to 1970), how can basic value-and-policy decisions be reached, say by 1985, while there is still enough room for us to maneuver and to defuse the catastrophes—as suggested in Figure 2—that could explode around our ears between the years 2000 and 2100?

**Hopeful Prospects for Survival and for Better Tomorrows.** In a positive vein, it is good to be able to report that most leaders in socio-technical research dealing with alternative futures and concerned with perceptive policy decisions are optimistic with respect to the fundamental power of human reason in skirting catastrophe by making prudent decisions. (Patently, without this level of confidence, there would be little if any point in futures research!)

These optimists believe that because of improving human knowledge and insights and with the help of applied, enlightened reason, accompanied by wiser use of technological know-how, much can be accomplished in the next five to twenty years to ameliorate our human problems. They point out, for instance, that in recent decades seminal ideas have begun to influence society quickly—in

**Figure 2:**
**A Computerized Projection of What Might Occur Between the**
**Present and the Year 2100 if Present Trends Continue**

- Natural resources down 75%
- Pollution exponential
- Seven billion drop (from ten billion) in population
- Industrial production declining due to lack of resources
- Per capita food production below the level of 1900

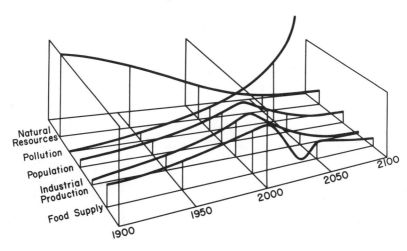

*Note:* The linear projections shown here were derived from a number of sources: Goesta Ehrensvaerd's estimates based on studies at The University of Lund in Sweden, the projections of Jay W. Forrester in *World Dynamics* and the Club of Rome Report, *The Limits of Growth*. The actual visualization was suggested by "Faut-il Stopper La Société de Consommation" in *Paris Match*, July, 1972. p. 40-57. We are indebted to Paul Peloquin for the crisp draftsmanship in this graph.

from ten to fifteen years—and that extraordinary goals such as the moon landings and orbiting space stations can be accomplished very quickly once determination, funding, and creative power are blended in the right proportions. Apparently, if we cannot persuade the genii of technology to return to the magic lamp, we can put him to work with a foresight that makes him the loyal servant he was intended to be!

Another development which brings a sense of security is the conclusion implicit in the recent history of science and technology that the impact of the changes they have brought may top out in the 1970s—and indeed are tapering off already. Consider the following diagrams, preserved from conversation with John Platt. In Figure 3 we see the exponential curve of technological change and a comparable curve of human and social problems which change created.

As the key on the model shows, one of the two lines

**Figure 3:**
**A Model of Hypothecated Paths Showing Technological Change Rates and Their Concomitant Social Problems**

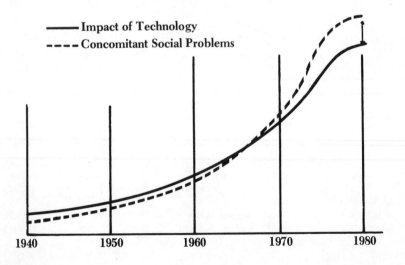

represents the exponential change rate of recent years. Without any pretense at mathematical precision, the "Impact of Technology" line is intended to symbolize the points that:

(1) Telecommunication is virtually instantaneous around the world. A $10^7$ increase in the speed of our transmission of visual images can, for practical purposes, become no faster.

(2) Since 1935, information data processing has increased by $10^6$, and further changes will not have a commensurate impact.

(3) Speed of travel, increases in the power from energy sources, and the rate of population increase have gone up a thousandfold to $10^2$. Further increases are not going to hit us much harder than they already have. The U.S. birth rate is at one of its lowest ebbs in history.

(4) The power of destruction, increased by $10^2$ since 1945, is already so great that we dare not contemplate using the weapons we have. More deadly ones are not likely to increase further the present threat of overkill.

(5) The rate of population increase has tripled in the last century, and the rate has increased about one thousandfold since the Paleolithic era. The densities of populations may have gone up several times in major cities. The numbers of human interactions [which vary with the square of the density] may have increased 10 to a 100 times [there is no accurate way to measure this].

(6) The power of weapons has increased $10^6$ times [one millionfold] since 1944, from 20-ton blockbusters to 20-megaton H-bombs.

The second line—"Concomitant Social Problems"—suggests that mankind's difficulties likewise have proliferated and that at some time in the mid-1960s they became more numerous even than the changes that bred them.

Figure 3 also reflects a serendipitous future development—the coming top-off of the impact of change on man and the consequent taper-off of humankind's social problems as the shock waves of change become less able to jar us. The diagram suggests that this could begin to occur in the mid-1970s.

As the model in Figure 3 is meant to suggest, we now have weapons too deadly for a sane head of state to use. Satellites have given us virtually instantaneous worldwide audiovisual communication, and travel in supersonic transports is so fast that after a London to Montreal flight in two hours on the Concorde, one's body almost needs to wait for his soul to catch up. Furthermore, the leap from coal to nuclear power has given us a thousandfold boost in energy resources. In short, after thirty years of cataclysmic developments, the *impact* of change on society between 1940 and 1970 seems more than likely to decrease. It is important to reiterate that it is the *impact* that should decline. It does not necessarily follow that the *rate* of change will top off in the 1970s and 1980s. Computerized data processing inevitably will become more rapid and more efficient, the federal income tax seine become more tightly woven, the use of credit cards become more widespread, and the speed with which plane reservations are verified even less error-prone. But these further changes are not as likely to enter and to mediate our way of life in the next ten or fifteen years to the same degree or to the same extent that they influenced us between 1955 or 1960 and 1970. Toffler's "future shock" can also be expected further to diminish as suggested by the bell-shaped line that has been added in Figure 4. Worldwide communication by satellite can't be any faster than instantaneous! Nor is there any new wallop in "super-overkill" weaponry when present "overkill" weapons are so deadly that the United States recently felt compelled to dispose of its biological warfare arsenal. As a result, as we learn to live with change, we should become less and less upset by Toffler's "dizzying disorientation brought on by the

premature arrival of the future" to which reference has
already been made.

So—say some thoughtful and persuasive policy researchers—we can expect to have a respite from dizzying
sociotechnical change: an interval during which to repair
our psychological balance and in which to consolidate
our gains in environment control while we try to find better
ways to heal the social wounds and sore spots created by
the portentous changes and dislocations of 1940-1970.

Figure 5 is a composite of the first three charts and
adds one other dimension. This is shown in the descend-
ing line drawn to denote a possible loss of sensitivity on
the part of persons in the United States. It is intended to
illustrate the point that mass production has diminished
our sensitivities to many amenities that were once enjoyed,
at least by people with middle-class and upper-class incomes in years gone by, when such persons could pur-

**Figure 4:**
**Model of the Impact of Change with the Phenomenon**
**of Future Shock Added**

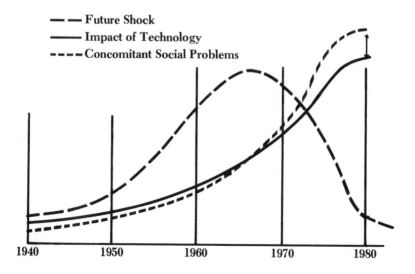

chase beautifully hand-crafted and individualized products: furniture, shoes, carefully prepared food, and so on.

Note, however, that the "sensitivity" line is shown as beginning to worm its way upward in the immediate future, perhaps as soon as two or three years hence. There are omens and portents that this is not merely wishful thinking—a point made in the scenarios of Chapter II.

**Ad Astra per Aspera.** The prescient citizens of Kansas long ago chose a state motto that seems relevant to humankind's prospects for the future: *Ad astra per aspera*— "To the stars the hard way." If we are reasonably willing to try to "make it the hard way," there is no real reason— other than the possibility of our own perversity and intransigeance—why we can't.

Sociologist Daniel Bell recently claimed that he had identified seven facts in the United States that threaten

**Figure 5:**
**Composite Model of Figures 3 and 4 With "Sensitivity Index"**
**and Selected Biotechnical and Social Change Added**

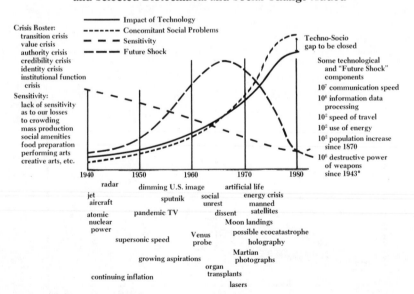

°Exponential estimates adapted from John Platt.

the present order: private violence such as political assassination, "insoluble" problems such as urban decay, governmental stalemates on such vital issues as economics versus human needs, social conflict, regional economic imbalances, alienation of the intelligensia, and military humiliation as in the U.S. withdrawal from Southeast Asia. No one of these, no combination of the seven, is irretreivably beyond repair, and some probably have diminished since Bell first listed them in the British journal *Encounter* three years back.

In similar vein, Konrad Lorenz has ticked off "deadly sins" of the 1970s: overpopulation, harming the environment, internecine commercial competition, indoctrination, and, paradoxically, the drive to break down all traditions, and a tendency to overuse knowledge and technology to avoid all unpleasant stimuli. Here again, progress is being made. The U.S. population is stabilizing, drastic measures to protect the biosphere are contemplated, careful study is underway as to how we can better use technology, and so on.

While it is fashionable in some quarters to view the human race with something between alarm and despair, I am sanguine with respect to tomorrow's world and the potential of education in that world. True, it probably will fall short of perfection while any of us are around—but the human track record is a good one. In a mere tick on eternity's clock the human *experiment*—an experiment that began in the warm seas millions of years ago—has become in the past 50,000 years the human *experience.*

As we surmounted our great watersheds we gradually learned to hold a hostile environment in check, to develop architecture, transportation and communication networks, agriculture, sophisticated concepts of government, the sciences, a literature—even to develop the concept of God, or, if one chooses to reject Him in a secular era, an awareness of conscience and morality. I think we shall continue to have a good track record despite the tough problems that futurists inventory.

A large measure of our success will probably reside in what education can do—education properly conceived and funded. Let us next direct our attention to educational changes and innovations that seem to be implicit or that are explicit in the systemic and holistic views of policy research specialists.

## FOOTNOTES

[1]Cf. "Split Views on America," *Time*, December 25, 1972. European Edition, p. 20.

[2]Harold G. Shane, "Looking to the Future: Reassessment of Educational Issues of the 1970's," *Phi Delta Kappan*, 54:326-327, January, 1973.

[3]Alvin Toffler, "The Future as a Way of Life," *Horizons*, Summer, 1965, p. 109.

[4]Dennis Gabor, *The Mature Society*, New York: Praeger Publishers, 1972, p. 3. (Italics in original.)

[5]Ward, Barbara and Dubos, Réné, *Only One Earth: The Care and Maintenance of a Small Planet*, New York: Norton, 1972, p. 30.

CHAPTER IV

# Learning Designs for Tomorrow

**Education for Tomorrow's World**

When I first tried to bring the educational concepts and constructs of professional futurists into focus, I was reminded of O. Henry's remark about Webster's dictionary: interesting, but not a very well connected document when one sat down to read it. Another difficulty resides in the fact that the farther one seeks to peer ahead, the more obscure tomorrow becomes. David C. MacMichael of the Educational Policy Research Center at Stanford expressed the problem very well:

> For all of its utility, the tree of alternative futures has its limitations. For one thing, the foliage is pretty damned thick. We can see the trunk of today clearly enough and we have a reasonably unrestricted view of the places higher up where the major branches begin to fork out, just a few years into the future. But beyond that clear sight is a little difficult and descriptions of the shape and direction and texture of the upper limbs—the more distant alternative futures—becomes less and less precise.

Despite the limitations that inhere in stitching together soft data and opinions, I have done my best to portray some of the directions in which U.S. education may go during the next five to fifteen years. The ideas presented reflect honestly and, I hope, clearly the nature of certain alternative futures toward which most participants in futures research believe that education should move. At the same time, it must be understood that the *total* pattern of educational change portrayed here is a collage developed by the writer: an interpretation inferred from the ideas of the more than eighty scientists, logicians, and mathematicians, as these ideas appear when adapted or transplanted to the educational community of elementary or secondary schools and to post-secondary education.

On the whole, the views of futurists were liberal but not of an activist-radical sort. Neither was there any substantial body of opinion that the schools were so ineffectual that the present educational system had to be scrapped and replaced with markedly different "neo-humanistic" or "deschooled" forms of teaching and learning. Nor was there any strong sentiment that "electronic packages" would soon greatly alter the basic nature of the educational environment in the immediate future. Rather, stress was on the need for educators to improve implementation of many of the nascent trends and ideas of merit that already were in existence; in a word, to *reform* rather than to *revolutionize* education.

Most futurists were optimistic about educators' and communities' ability to reform the schools. Their main concern resided in the question of whether basic changes would occur as rapidly as circumstances required. If substantial changes such as are presented here actually materialize, then, the educational universe of the 1980s should be profoundly different from that of the 1960s and early 1970s.

**Changes That Suggest Themselves in U.S. Education.** What are some of the appealing changes that policy research specialists in the United States suggest should be explored by educational leadership? Let us look first at major focal points. These are: (1) clarification of *goals*, (2) changes in the *structure* or organization of the school, and (3) possible changes and additions or replacements in *subject matter*. Each of these three points will be considered in turn in the sections that follow.

### The Need for Clear, New Social and Educational Goals

At least since the early years of the century, U.S. schools have been characterized by a wide spectrum of both academic and humane goals. More often than not, these goals failed to coincide. Even when the humane and the academic objectives were similar (e.g., "Schooling should help the child learn how to think"), the means employed to attain the end were likely to be almost totally different.

Actually, our problem has not been the *lack* of educational objectives in curriculum guides and textbooks but a *surfeit* of conflicting or ambiguous statements. Some were subject matter goals; others ranged from broad human development and life adjustment to ambitious approaches involving social reform and help for the gifted and for the disadvantaged. By the mid-1960s, a strong and costly educational investment had become conspicuously overburdened with tasks dictated by goals that often were both too numerous and too conflicting for the schools to accomplish. Problems and disagreements extended from early childhood education through the post-secondary level.

**The Increased Importance of Goals.** At the present juncture, most policy and futures research specialists agree that one of the nation's tasks is to determine what it really seeks in the decades ahead and what these aspirations mean for the schools. Lacking some form of social consensus as to what it should accomplish, U.S. education will remain in deeply troubled waters. This is because our schools are not independent agencies but function as an integral part of the culture as a whole. As noted in Chapter III, schools reflect the social scene. Furthermore, with the possible exception of some programs designed for younger children, the social scene for which young learners are prepared is an unreal one, and one that fails to allow for the massive transitions of the past forty years.

The need for new, clear goals is heightened because twenty years of increasing affluence in the United States has entrenched our appetite for more material gains for more people. We have moved from wistfully *longing* for a better living in the 1930s to *hoping* for a better quality of life in the late 1940s, to *expecting* greater material and human gains in the 1950s and to *demanding* them since the mid-1960s. The deterioration of the environment as a result of the accelerating quest for more goods, better services, more education, and greater mobility for all Americans has been extensively documented and poses some of the major paradoxes and problems of the 1970s. Major changes are inescapable. We now need to reassess our levels of social, material, and educational aspirations, futures research tells us, as we determine what the biosphere can provide, and to identify new, equitable, humane yet realistic levels of aspiration toward which we can afford to move.

**Building an Educational Foundation for Coping with Alternative Futures.** One of the dilemmas of the present, as implied above, resides in the fact that society is both ambivalent and ambiguous in its aspirations and in its ideas as to how schooling can best serve them. The confusion need not and should not, however, serve as a pretext for postponing certain basic reforms. Even while society comes to grips with the decisions that the times require, our schools can begin the task of studying and modifying or replacing educational doctrines and practices that have become of diminished value through the past thirty or forty years.

The development of new educational futures for young learners, for example, does not imply any loss of respect for substantive content. No policies research specialist would propose that there is a substitute for being able to read and to interpret the nuances of the printed page. A suitable foundation does, however, imply changes in the *climate* of learning as well as new and expanded approaches to content. Examples of some specific suggestions from futurists that promise to help children and youth better to cope with alternative futures:

(1) Provision, before as well as after birth, for careful physical and mental examination plus appropriate follow-up.
(2) Experiences, beginning with birth, that promise to create desirable cumulative cognitive input, with methodical schooling beginning no later than age three.
(3) Emphasis on a "personalized" program, which concentrates on the learner's optimum development rather than merely focusing on attempts to bring him up to group norms.
(4) Careful efforts to build in the student a positive view of himself—so that he does not feel he is "dirty," "stupid," a "nonreader," and so on.
(5) Development of a suitable future-focused role image (FFRI), a point already mentioned. This is analogous to the self-concept, but extends forward through time to delineate a realistic, *motivating* concept of the options he has in working toward a life-role that brings satisfaction and promises self-respect and dignity.
(6) Endeavor, even with quite young (ten-twelve years old) children, to study the "history of the future." Help them through old magazines, books, and papers, for instance, to see how "today" was foreshadowed eight or ten years ago, study how the neighborhood has changed in four to eight years. What caused these changes? Were they desirable ones? What was done—or not done—to bring about change? How do we go about the task of looking ahead? How does one identify alternative futures and prepare promising scenarios?
(7) Identify ways in which children and youth can be-

come of greater value to the community through work-service programs—through "action learning"— sponsored by the school and involving adults in the vicinity. (The purpose here is again to involve children in some of the useful work roles many of them might have filled had they been alive prior to 1920 or 1930 and which gave them a sense of worth.) Cleaning litter on beaches or parks or taking care of school clean-up needs are examples of non-exploitive jobs in which even six- or eight-year olds could engage. Older children and youth could perform many more forms of socially useful work, for example, by serving as pre-paraprofessionals helping in programs for children of five and under, tutoring other children, operating teaching aids in school, or helping to prepare and distribute food provided through welfare programs. This approach could well eventuate in more widespread postponement of post-secondary education, perhaps decrease the relative number of persons seeking a baccalaureate degree, yet more firmly motivate those who do seek to enter a field of work that requires academic credentials.

(8) Utilize the community itself as a huge teaching aid by means of which many learnings could transpire. In effect, this implies making the community environment not an *alternative* school but a more meaningful *adjunct* to schooling.

The eight broad points above are intended to suggest the nature of educational programs that successfully enable youth effectively to mesh itself with any of a number of alternative futures that lie ahead. Surely, such programs will need to depart sharply from contemporary schooling practices that are predominantly passive, didactic, and cloistered within conventional classroom walls. In short, the proposed changes would profoundly transform the present school environment experienced in childhood, but without dismantling or wrecking the present educational community.

There is no reason to believe that desirable educational changes cannot be made within the infrastructure of U.S. schools. The futurist's emphasis is on reformation and renewal rather than on demolition or revolution. Let us now examine some general characteristics of educational reform to be attained through wise choices among tomorrow's alternative possibilities.

### A Proposed Infrastructure for Unifying U.S. Education

What kind of changes in the organizational structure of U.S. education are suggested by the images of the future to which a number of policies research specialists appear to subscribe? What does an extrapolation of their writings and research projects suggest?

As one examines the survey data and their implications for a new organizational structure, four points seem clear:

(1) The infrastructure of U.S. education should be much more flexible; be less hampered by doctrinaire or "red-tape" regulations.

(2) The deployment of instructional personnel should be more imaginative, more varied, and involve greater interaction with the community and with one's colleagues as well as with more transactions among both teachers and learners at more widespread age levels.

(3) Deliberate, methodical provisions should be made for education beginning in early childhood and extending into old age.

(4) The structural matrices for learning should become more permeated by the third force or humanistic psychology associated with writers such as the late Abraham H. Maslow.

In the realm of subject matter, which is discussed later in the present chapter, futures research stresses seven points, namely:

(1) That there should be continued powerful stress on the acquisition of meaningful substantive content,

but that "content" should be more broadly defined in U.S. schools of the late 1970s.

(2) That there should be less uniformity in what substantive content is acquired by a given learner.

(3) That the time at which individual learners encounter similar ideas, content, and concepts should vary appreciably.

(4) That more expressive and affective experiences should be introduced to lend better balance to instrumental and cognitive emphasis in the curriculum, and that the cognitive should more often be *approached* through the affective domain.

(5) That despite an increased aura of permissiveness, the freedoms enjoyed should be freedom *to* accomplish, *to* learn, and *to* produce—not freedom *from* responsibility or *from* the need for the individual to contribute.

(6) That changes will need to be made in current incentive and reward structures so that teachers and students alike—at all educational levels—will be motivated to adapt themselves to new and broadened interpretations and concepts of performance, achievement, and "success."

(7) Finally, that practice should more widely precede theory; that ideas and procedures should be tried out as one of the processes *antecedent* to becoming accepted educational theory.

With this preamble, attention now turns to a description of a modified organizational structure of the schools that appears to permeate the suggestions of many policies researchers.

**A Rationale for Structural Change in U.S. Schools.** Changes in the infrastructure of public education, as suggested by our survey interviews, would move the schools toward the vitalizing idea of a lifelong educational continuum of schooling. It would be somewhat more complex than current organizational plans because of its widened scope and lengthened sequence and because of its variability and flexibility. But such a continuum should be easier to administer because of the increased autonomy of individual units. It also should quickly become apparent to the reader that many of the ideas embodied in a lifelong continuum are not novel ones. Many of the pieces of the infrastructure are already in place in a small number of schools, and all of the pieces are on the inventory list of U.S. educational ideas. The contribution of the structure that emerges below lies in the *Gestalt* that it creates, the new panorama of perceptions that have not heretofore been seen in a clear interrelationship.

The rationale for abandonment of the graded structure that is generally found in present-day schools in favor of a smoothly flowing, seamless continuum can be stated as follows:

(1) Human beings are unique, grow and learn at different rates, have accumulated quite different bodies of experiential input, and have diverse self-concepts and role images with respect to the future. Furthermore, when exposed to the same experiences, because of their uniquely personalized backgrounds, no two learners see and hear the same thing—*and their neurosystems may actually record totally different inputs*. Therefore, schooling should acknowledge the fact of these differences and drop the "impossible dream" of seeking to bring children and youth up to arbitrary and uniform standards of academic and social performance.

(2) Learning is continuous, and reasons for a nine-month September-June school year have lost whatever validity they once may have had. With appropriate physical changes such as air conditioning for schools located in warm areas, we should be able to modify programs to permit children to attend for a total of 180 to 200 days, but spread throughout the year. The actual timing of attend-

ance would be determined by professional judgment, family circumstances, efficient use of the school environment, and the future development of teaching materials such as TV cassettes that can be used at home.

(3) Education, and the need for some type of experiences that schools can provide, extends throughout life. There are human needs at forty, sixty, and even well past age seventy that are as real as they are at age five or fifteen or twenty-five. There are needs for new skills as technosocial changes emerge, and for new knowledge in fields in which one studied a quarter of a century before. Also there are the steadily growing challenges of the constructive use of leisure, of preparation for post-retirement careers as life spans lengthen, and, of course, for interests and activities that can be encouraged and thus make old age something less than a disease to be dreaded.

On the basis of the rationale presented above, in what type of infrastructure do a substantial number of policy research specialists see merit?

**Uninterrupted Educational Progress in a Seamless Continuum.** Perhaps a simple statement, accompanied by uncomplicated models, is the best means of capturing the educational significance of lifelong opportunities for learning and of depicting the idea of a seamless continuum. Let us begin with education for the youngest.

**Early Childhood Education.** Although a seamless curriculum has no conventional segments, such as "pre-school" or "middle school," such familiar terms are used here to facilitate communication and to convey more readily an understanding of the learner's progress through a continuum.

The outset of lifelong learning opportunities would begin with the child's first direct contacts with the educational community somewhere near the date of his second birthday. Let us call this the *nonschool preschool* experience. This early introduction to the school would include obtaining data from physical and mental examinations, compiling background information, and so on. The nonschool preschool interval also would provide a beginning for computerized cumulative record forms for what might become a nationwide student data bank, although only if confidentiality can be guaranteed.

Depending on his maturity, direct instructional contact with a school program would begin near a child's third birthday. At this point he would, for half-days, enter a *minischool* group of six or eight other three-year-olds. This cluster of experiences quite probably would be directed by a paraprofessional who, in turn, was supervised (along with six or eight other paraprofessionals) by a teacher-consultant with full credentials and experience. Work in the minischool would be educational rather than custodial, carried forward on a "developmental" basis— one deliberately designed to provide socialization and rich cognitive input. This input is gaining greater importance as it becomes recognized that meaningful experiences may very well be the raw material of what is subsequently measured as intelligence. This does not, however, imply a need to provide early "academic" experience in, say, reading or mathematics.

When he is approximately four in the seamless curriculum a child would find himself transposed[1] to the *pre-primary component* of the curriculum. He would move from the minischool when deemed ready, not at a set calendar date. Administratively, the change would be analogous to the processes involved when mid-semester transfer pupils appear in a new classroom because their parents have moved to a different school district. Furthermore, the pre-primary period proposed here is not the same as most contemporary four- and five-year-old kindergartens. It would be more of an *educational* "ready-room" than a *custodial* "romper-room;" a learning center with methodical input rather than a custodial center merely featuring supervised care and entertainment in a safe, plastic environmental bubble.

During the variable interval that a child spent in the pre-primary continuum, empathizing teachers would create an interesting, challenging climate, and help each student to reach an optimum point of development before his transition into the program designed for him during the primary years. The fast-learning and mature, perhaps two or three youngsters out of a total of fifty, might move from the primary continuum into the primary school in as little time as one year, and as early as at age five, to work with children of six or seven. Conversely, some boys and girls (among them the physically handicapped, the disadvantaged, culturally deprived, or slow maturing) might need to invest their time in three or even four make-ready years and postpone any extensive work with six- or seven-year-olds until they were eight and occasionally even nine.

During the primary years, which are conceived to be an integral part of a continuum beginning in early childhood, most children would be from six to nine years of age. But the groups in which they work would *not* be based on chronological age. Instead they would be ephemeral groupings built around emergent projects involving inquiry, exploratory, expressive, and cognitive ventures in which a varied mix of ages would be found—just as such children now work or play in informal, neighborhood groups.

**The Flow of Learning During the Middle School Years.** In the seamless curriculum, the pupil would move without interruption, from the primary continuum to the middle school continuum. The transposition would occur at whatever time during an unbroken school year that it became apparent (in the professional judgment of the faculty) that a young learner was ready to function in a predominantly nine- to twelve-year age range rather than in a predominantly six- to nine-year age cluster or pod. In some instances, where children in the middle school years and primary years are housed in the same building, the child's translation or transposition to older working groups would be virtually undiscernible. In other instances, depending on the physical plant, a change from one building to another would be involved, but it should occur with a minimum of fuss or fanfare.

The governing principles suggested for the primary continuum would tend to prevail in the middle school continuum. In this span of approximately three years, the learner would spend from as little as two years to as many as five. (See Figure 6.) The concepts of double promotion or "skipping" would totally disappear, however. So would the retardation practice of "flunking." In a personalized continuum, one would move at his own speed without reference to group norms.[2] In the process, over a period of time, the age range of children in the primary and middle school phases of the continuum would and should extend so that eventually the elementary age range would be not from six to twelve years as at present, but would extend from five- to fifteen-year-oldness—exclusive of programs for early childhood groups ranging from age two or three to ages five and six. It should be understood, however, that an increase in the age range would not proportionately increase the range in ability. The continuum approach would actually tend to decrease the four-to-eight-year range in performance found in, say, a present-day fourth grade group.[3] Over a period of years in the continuum school, ability referenced rather than chronologically referenced groups would emerge.

**New Secondary School Concepts: The Paracurriculum.** Although the more highly structured content of many secondary schools would require some adjustments, the idea of uninterrupted progress could and should carry over to and continue in the high school phase. This would involve careful guidance of the individual learner, abandonment of many rigid contemporary requirements for admission, for exit, and for re-entry and require considerable re-education on the part of those teachers who are predominantly subject and semester minded. Improving educational technologies, the development of more sophis-

Figure 6:
Model of the Seamless Curriculum: An Emerging School Structure for the 1980s

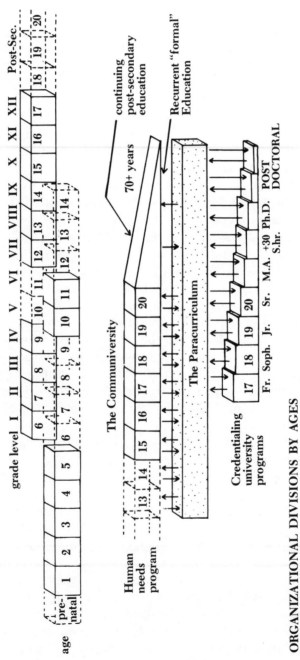

ORGANIZATIONAL DIVISIONS BY AGES

2   Nonschool preschool
3   Minischool
4-5   Pre-primary continuum
6-9   Primary continuum

10-13   Upper and lower middle school
14-20+   Secondary-community college continuum
15-70+   University and post-secondary continuum

Numbers in each
cube refer to the
learner's approximate age.

ticated programmed materials, and the increased use of differentiated staffing seem likely to ease many problems in the gradual transition to a continuum at the early and middle adolescent levels.

The most formidable impediment to changes in the secondary school program is likely to be found in the minds of some teachers, parents, and administrators. Even those who quickly accept the merit of the seven points on subject matter are likely to need considerable convincing and re-education with respect to cross-disciplinary approaches to subject matter, the flexible "teaching partnership" concept, and teaching to develop desired attitudes and values in addition to subject matter content *per se.*

One of the most interesting but little discussed and least explored developments implicit in the continuum is the concept of the paracurriculum and its implications for major modifications in the compulsory education laws presently found in many states in the union. *The paracurriculum concept recognizes that schooling provides only a part of the experiential input that adds up to the learner's education.* Indeed, in many instances the nonschool learnings of children and youth may be by far the most extensive (and sometimes the most valuable) components or factors in helping him to cope with, to manipulate, and to control his environment.

Before continuing further, the term "paracurriculum" should be defined more explicitly. The word refers to the body of out-of-school experiences that help to strengthen the intellectual ability, general background, and coping powers of the child or youth. To whatever extent possible, secondary and post-secondary education institutions should deliberately plan to make greater and more deliberate use of the paracurriculum. As shown by the model in Figure 7, the paracurriculum—the world of nonschool experiences for which the school is participatory planner and for which it serves as a broker—parallels the curriculum as the name obviously suggests. As is illustrated by the model, the paracurriculum involves world-of-work experiences, sometimes without but usually with pay, which temporarily or permanently replace in-school activities.

As conceived here, the paracurriculum concept might be implemented as follows:

(1) At age fifteen, perhaps even as early as age thirteen in rare instances, a student for whom it is judged appropriate could engage in a useful vocational activity without attending school.

(2) His lateral move from the world of the school to the "real world," as implied in the model, would be arranged or "brokered" by the school. This process would involve teachers' professional judgments, in-depth counseling, parental understanding, consent, support, and cooperation, and close working relationships with employers who are socially minded and willing to offer their enterprises as alternatives to conventional schooling without exploiting fourteen- to sixteen-year-old worker-learners.

(3) The paracurriculum would eliminate "push-outs" and dropouts. One simply does not drop out of an educational continuum; he moves at a 90 degree angle (see model) into planned paracurricular learnings and continues his education in what, hopefully, will be an experience of increased educational significance.

(4) An integral part of the paracurriculum is the privilege of infinite, methodically planned lifelong exit and re-entry privileges carefully coordinated through enlightened guidance practices. (See arrows in Figure 6.) The planned re-entry is an indispensable ingredient. Lacking this ingredient, an early leaving age re-opens the Pandora's box of child labor and exploitation of the disadvantaged.

(5) The continuum of schooling and the paracurriculum are portrayed as being almost as intimately related as Siamese twins, and both deeply involve the strong and enlightened effort of the educational

community. By age fourteen, after approximately a decade of guided, personalized progress, the early adolescent would be helped to move from curriculum to paracurriculum *and vice versa* without problems and without any clinging stigma. Furthermore, with graded structures abandoned, there would no longer be an eighth-grade group or a sophomore class from which to withdraw. Age ranges, greatly increased by the flexible and often ephemeral and functional approaches to grouping, would also make exit and re-entry inconspicuous and matter-of-fact as in graduate study where persons in their early twenties may rub shoulders with students twice their age.

(6) As envisioned here, the paracurricular concept is not a limited innovation applicable at the early adolescent level. Rather, it is part of the total warp and woof of lifelong education. It is applicable even in early childhood in the form of simple community service contributions (e.g., keeping a park or playground clean) and in the learner's later maturity when, perhaps at sixty, he returns from the paracurricular to the curricular realm with the hope of making his retirement more meaningful or a post-retirement job more feasible through his further education.

Despite the novel organizational configuration of the paracurricular concept, it is made up of components that have already been discussed and sometimes introduced on the U.S. educational scene under such labels as "socially useful work," "continuing education," or "paid internships." If and as the idea of a seamless, lifelong, year-around educational continuum gains acceptance, the paracurricular concept might well become a viable and important concomitant source—a kind of launching pad—for many alternative approaches to learning in our educational futures. It clearly reflects the idea that we do not need alternatives *to* schools, so much as we need more imaginative alternatives *within* the established educational community.

**Post-Secondary Education.** Our résumé of possible changes in the infrastructure of U.S. education, as inferred from futures research, now is described with reference to the final phase of the continuum: the post-secondary phase, including, of course, the university but also embracing forms of noncollegiate post-secondary learning resources.

As shown in Figure 7, a reproduction of Figure 6, the post-secondary student might either be a person who had completed four years of secondary (curricular) education or someone who had been continuing his education in world-of-work (paracurricular) activities. In either case, he would not be deprived of access to, or of the opportunity to complete, whatever components of education that brought him personal satisfaction or increased the likelihood of vocational success.

Also notice in Figure 7 that "secondary" and "post-secondary" education are depicted as an uninterrupted continuum. They are paralleled by the lifelong paracurriculum and intimately interlinked by infinite exit and re-entry privileges, which insure that no one at any age is deprived of post-secondary educational opportunities from which he believes he can profit.

**Figure 7:**
**Model of an Educational Continuum: The Curricular-**
**Paracurricular Relationship in Their Secondary and**
**Post-Secondary Phases**

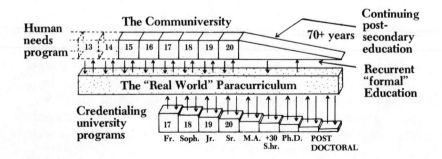

As noted in the enlarged model, a distinction is made in the proposed infrastructure of the continuum between secondary/post-secondary education and credentialed university or professional education. Presumably, for the foreseeable future, the culture will maintain levels of study leading to advanced certificates or degrees and continue to rely on certification or similar credentials in an effort to insure that persons are qualified—insofar as laboratories, examinations, classrooms, clinics, and supervised experiences can qualify them—to enter a given professional or service field.[4]

The section representing post-secondary education is also intended to portray a growing recognition in the future of the need for persons of forty, sixty, or older to be able to participate either steadily or periodically in many forms of what was known as adult education, continuing education, or "night school" in past decades. The main differences in provisions for lifelong post-secondary education as depicted here reside in:

(1) *Imaginative and relevant changes in the curricular and paracurricular offerings at the post-secondary level including not only new, pertinent community college or communiversity programs, but also changes in the secondary program.* In keeping with the "seamless continuum" concept, for the purposes of mature learners,[5] *all* educational resources should be open to them on a noncredit basis, with the prerogative of taking examinations if they decide later to seek credit for advanced study in the credentialing channel at the bottom of the model. (Cf. Figure 7.)

(2) *Gradual but fundamental changes in certain contemporary practices in the liberal arts college and in its image.* In effect, the present-day four-year arts and science component of the university would *become* the communiversity, but with appreciably expanded purpose, scope, and noncredit enrollment.

While retaining much of their traditional content and general education function, arts and science offerings, much content would be expanded or modified to meet the needs of more learners of all ages and would "find room in the folds of their academic robes" for every viable form of post-secondary learning to which learners aspired.

It should be clearly understood that the liberal arts would neither be abandoned nor diluted. However, as in Britain's Open University program, no one would be denied access to higher education if he were seriously motivated to do work either with or without academic credit. The proposal suggests new emphasis on, and recognition for, teaching and service activities of the faculty in addition to the present reward system for research and scholarship.

(3) *A flexible viewpoint regarding grouping for learning as well as for creating a psychological climate for learners of a much wider age-range.* Teachers at the secondary and communiversity levels as well as in the university need to become adjusted to working with qualified learners of virtually all ages as the multiple exit and re-entry concept penetrates educational practice. A precedent—as noted earlier—may be found in university graduate study where, in a given class or seminar, persons in their early twenties may rub shoulders with individuals thirty years their seniors.

(4) *Ways must be explored to permit mature learners to return as "come-backs" or "drop-ins," a reversal of the present dropout phenomenon.* This involves co-operative, enlightened policy planning by industry, government, and education. Job security, imaginative financial provisions, and changes in employment and retirement policies are a few of the elements that seem certain to be involved in lifelong learning opportunities.

The modified organizational infrastructure that has been briefly described above is not capable of existing—nor is it even possible to create—without certain substantial changes in the deployment of teachers in all fields of endeavor. What are the new needs and possibilities in teachers' roles that seem to be congruent with the research and thinking in the realm of futures studies?

**Staff Deployment.** Among alternative educational futures is the possibility that the current concept of team teaching needs to be extended or at least appreciably modified to develop even more versatile and flexible "teaching partnerships," especially if an educational continuum is introduced on a widening scale. The teaching partnership concept is depicted in Figure 8, which follows.

Although the model illustrates a teaching partnership as it might appear in the primary or middle school phases of a seamless educational continuum, the basic ideas are applicable even in a departmental structure at the university level. This approach to staff deployment involves:

(1) The basic idea of differentiated staffing with a "senior partner," with certificated teachers (numbers 1-4), with paraprofessionals (P) serving as teacher aides, and with residents (R) who are fully qualified teachers either in their first or second year or more mature teachers returning, after some years of absence, to ready themselves for participation in new instructional roles.[6]

(2) Since the "continuum school" presumably would operate on a twelve-month year, it would employ more teachers, aides, and residents than actually are on duty at a given time. This point is depicted by the "X," "Y," and "Z" enclosed by broken lines. The "X," for instance, symbolizes a teacher who does not have a classroom duty assignment during a given time interval. He may be absent but working on a curriculum or materials preparation assignment, engaging in professional study or research,

Figure 8:
Model of the Teaching Partnership and its Associated Support Systems

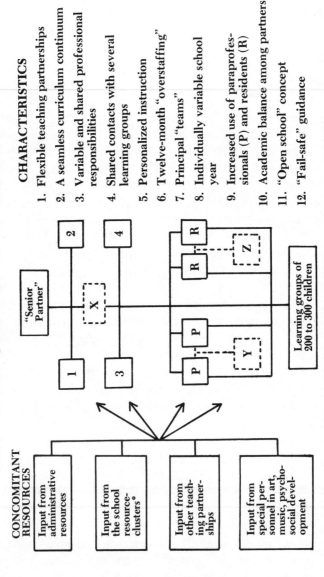

CHARACTERISTICS

1. Flexible teaching partnerships
2. A seamless curriculum continuum
3. Variable and shared professional responsibilities
4. Shared contacts with several learning groups
5. Personalized instruction
6. Twelve-month "overstaffing"
7. Principal "teams"
8. Individually variable school year
9. Increased use of paraprofessionals (P) and residents (R)
10. Academic balance among partners
11. "Open school" concept
12. "Fail-safe" guidance

*Resource-cluster components might include: (1) a guidance center, (2) computer facilities, (3) materials development staff, (4) instructional systems-technology cadre, (5) biochemeducationists, (6) Human Relations Center, (7) S-R (Self-Realization) Center, (8) Evaluation-assessment and Performance Analysis Center.

or taking some vacation or leave time. With appropriate modifications, the same generalizations apply to teacher's aide "Y" and to resident "R."

(3) As suggested by Figure 8, the "teaching partnership approach" influences staff deployment on a wider basis than the flexible teaching cluster, *per se*. In other words, a modified approach is needed to the assignment of other personnel. The lefthand column, "Concomitant Resources," suggests staffing strategies such as administrative resources in the form of principal teams. Instead of working on a one-principal-to-one-building basis, a team of, say, four persons could serve as special leadership consultants in four buildings, plan as a cooperative group, and spend their time as professional judgment dictated. All four might be in one building for a week, for example, or be engaged in any number of individual variations of time-investment. An analagous approach could be employed at the communiversity and university when as interdepartmental and interdisciplinary programs continue to develop as "area studies."

(4) Various characteristics of the teaching partnership are listed to the right of the model. They serve as a summary of various qualities of the seamless curriculum mentioned earlier and that have a bearing on the differentiated staffing in the partnership.

Like an ancient Gaelic or Greek triskelion, the seamless curriculum has three branches. We have discussed possible developments in the infrastructure and changes in staff deployment. Now what do policies research specialists have to say about changes in the content of instruction during the coming decade?

## Subject Matter for 1975-1985
**Instructional Perceptions of Futurists.** As one might logically infer, futures research personnel were deeply in-

terested in educating children and youth to develop the ability (1) to recognize and to select wisely among alternative futures, (2) to develop skills—including "process" skills—needed to implement their pursuit of desirable futures, and (3) to devise motivating experiences that would prompt young learners to become as realistic as possible, both in their views and in their efforts to work for a more viable society both in the United States and internationally.

These three aims, presumably, would permeate or at least influence the selection and design of subject matter for a seamless, personalized curriculum and paracurriculum. At the same time, educational futurists felt that it was the prerogative of professional educationists to determine policies. As a result, they expressed relatively few highly specific ideas regarding the scope, sequence, timing, and pacing of what was taught. To put it concisely, most policy decision personnel advocated reforms in conventional education without prescribing many precise new practices.

In general, however, there was agreement on the broad aims to be sought through instruction, warm acceptance of the need for schooling to develop moral and emotional strengths, to improve physical wellbeing, and to nurture cognitive power. As might have been expected among a scholarly group (a large majority of the survey participants had at least one earned doctorate), there was great respect for an education to insure mastery over whatever skills an individual could achieve mastery. But there was also widespread recognition of the point that many different ceilings-of-academic-achievement for individual human beings should be recognized in both the curriculum and in the paracurriculum. As a consequence, according to futurists, schooling in the United States needs to reverse its present stubborn and obsolete practice of over-emphasizing the fancied socioeconomic and social status advantages to be gained by entering vocations associated with professional, managerial, ownership, or executive-type roles. Conversely, not enough stress is being placed on the dignity and importance of all kinds of labor with hands as well as minds or on the many kinds of technical jobs open to persons without a college degree.

The typical futures research person emerged as an "idealist" in the sense of seeking curriculum content for better alternative futures and as a "realist" in the sense that he saw a continued need to maintain certain long-established academic goals, firm rather than harsh intellectual discipline, fair but not unreasonable or harshly demanding standards for individual accomplishment, and the need for mastery of substantive content on the part of those whose contributions to society would thereby be increased.

**Emerging Characteristics of Curricular Content Designed for the Future.** Rather than radical changes in the nature of what was taught, futures researchers felt that major changes were required in what was emphasized in a seamless curriculum. What many of them believe should receive more emphasis was, by the way, signaled in Chapter III, which dealt with social problems that a majority of futurists deemed to be critical. Let us look at plausible new content and emphases based on inferences drawn from interview data but not focused on specific content in a given subject.

*First,* and perhaps foremost, stress would be placed upon regaining, in enlightened form, the social discipline that gave Western man and perhaps most of mankind a sense of direction before the present value crisis. That crisis, with its relativism and permissive qualities, interferred with the steady whirl of the culturally imposed "inner gyroscope" that provided a course for the individual to follow—or at least to refer to—earlier in the present century. This effort should not be interpreted to imply a retreat to old, outmoded values, but an *advance* toward new values and life styles that are needed on our threatened planet.

*Second,* through education, an assault would be made on the strongly cemented redoubts of materialism; most specifically on the culture's misplaced confidence in mate-

rialism—in "consumer stuff"—as the most important goal of
life. As David Riesman once noted, the morale of even a
meritocracy can be ". . . undermined because its scientific
and rationalist temper has no religious basis and the system no transcendent aims, no goal beyond its own further
advance." Policy decision specialists would appear to agree
that material goods in themselves leave the deeper long-
ings of the human spirit or psyche unsatisfied and can sur-
round us with more and more ecological threats unless—
through education—we direct attention to changing our
"thing-centered" values and heretofore unchecked appetite
for consumer goods. As one West Coast policies specialist
(quoting Oscar Wilde) put it, we need to stop turning out
millions of youth "who know the price of everything and
the value of nothing."

   *Third*, the dangers and problems of the naive use of
technology (as powerfully presented by Barry Commoner
when he portrays problems in our ecosphere) would provide
appreciable content.[7] The attitudes uniformly expressed
during the survey not only supported the importance of
technology in bettering man's lot in most parts of the world,
but also reflected the overwhelming need, through the
prudent use of technology, to ease the problems of un-
thinking use of *La Technique*, as Jacques Ellul called it.
At all age levels, as has repeatedly been noted, the need
to rethink the use made of technology could be injected
into the curriculum.

   *Fourth*, and closely related to point three above, the
curriculum should begin to respond more adequately to
the threat of damage to the biosphere; damage that could
be profound and irreversible in a decade or two. Already, some futurists feel, the present flush of prosperity
and even affluence in industrially developed nations is only
a mask for pending global catastrophe. While few if any
are as pessimistic as Paul Ehrlich, or as harsh as William
and Paul Paddock in *Famine 1975*, all probably would
agree that:
   Since the environmental crisis is the result of the social

mis-management of the world's resources, then it can be resolved and man can survive in a humane condition when the social organization of man is brought into harmony with the ecosphere.[8]

Patently, education would have an important role here when and if major social decisions are reached with respect to national policy—and in any case there is a great deal of groundwork to be begun in the schools during the interval 1974-1980!

*Fifth*, since it was recognized as a major problem in Chapter III, most futurists apparently would like to see the schools face up to the fact that in the United States there is no really satisfactory coping doctrine for a major and almost totally ignored dilemma of democracy: Most Americans are unwilling to settle for a merely egalitarian society. Instead, they view "democracy" as a social order in which they are free to gamble on attaining "equality" with the top 10 percent, not as a means of attaining equity for all. Many of the concepts of the Founding Fathers have so far managed to survive because of political ingenuity, compromise, and the ability of the social establishment heretofore to accommodate a great deal of upward mobility. But education in the next decade may need to emphasize concepts of greater equity in democracy and discard the dream that everyone can rise above his father's status in life. This has implication not only for guidance counselors but for all teachers who are still selling the Horatio Alger myth.

At the risk of hearing cries of heresy, it seems essential that we reverse some of our long-ingrained ideas and vigorously emphasize that "success" does not necessarily reside in the nineteenth-century dictum that the able child should rise above his father's station in life. With social conditions and social attitudes changing (and with chemists, engineers, psychologists, lawyers, teachers, anthropologists, *et al.* unemployed or underemployed), there appears to be new and great merit in school climates—and in mass media—that would encourage some cobblers' sons to remain cobblers' sons, lest we end up unshod a few years hence.

*Sixth,* education needs to continue to sensitize the learner to the problems and to the neo-Malthusian dangers in unrestricted breeding. Futurists vary as to dates at which the problem might become catastrophic, but there is almost universal agreement that education for population control is imperative. One gloomy estimate by the Scandinavian scientist, Ehrensvaerd, is that beginning in 2050 the world population will shrink from over ten billion to three billion. The latter figure represents all the people that the diminished resources of the world can sustain in 2070 if present rates of consumption and increases in consumption are projected. He concludes that over seven billion people might die off (2020 to 2050 A.D.) in the process of stabilizing population at the 1970 figure of three billion.

*Seventh,* and last, a number of futures researchers doubtless would urge new educational input to assist learners to cope with the potential power of mass media in shaping opinions and attitudes. Also, the post-elementary curriculum would be shaped by the study of possible dangers in mind control by other means (e.g., chemical and electrical stimuli) in addition to television, radio, or publications.

**Controversial New Dimensions in Content and in Instruction: 1975-1985.** If the data cited by futurists—and their accompanying recommendations—are taken seriously, we are likely to find that the processes of curriculum change related to the content or instruction are packed with dynamite. Let me explore a few of the implicit and explicit changes that the future may very well demand.

(1) *Presenting the concept of the "true-costing" of consumer goods.* We do not repay the biosphere at present for what our consumer goods *really* cost. Consider a subcompact automobile selling for, say, $2,500 F.O.B. Detroit. If the cost of *reclaiming* the metal from the chassis and body, the lead from the battery, the copper and aluminum from cooling system, air conditioner, and motor are added,

if the buyer is charged for final demolition that will eliminate wasteful and unsightly auto graveyards—in short, if every effort is made to restore the land from which the automobile (or refrigerator or electric washer) was wrenched, the cost of capital consumer goods probably would double. But we would be postponing the evil of the day when large areas of the planet will have been stripped naked as the moon. The crucial new curriculum issue is pretty obvious. Shall we begin to face up to the educational implications of diminishing resources?

(2) *Interpreting to youth the growing need to reverse our "growth-is-good" doxology in favor of the need for "dynamic contraction."* Thus far, aside from suspending judgment on the SST and the Alaskan oil pipelines, there is little evidence the people in the United States are willing even to *suspend* their attacks on the biosphere—let alone begin to do with less of its riches. The ineluctable truth is that sooner or later, we will need to contemplate instructing young learners as to the importance of *dynamic contraction,* a carefully planned withdrawal from our policy of fueling the economy with more of everything each year.

It simply doesn't make sense, for instance, to talk of producing twelve to fifteen million internal combustion cars in 1980 or in 1985 while our Environmental Protective Agency contemplates gas rationing in California a year or two hence because of smog-breeding exhaust emissions, and when gasoline itself has been in short supply.

Dynamic contraction, a recent concept in economics, concerns itself with such questions as how an overextended airline can reduce its size and be healthier through a loss of mechanized avoirdopois. Or how a transition from a one-or-two car per family economy can be changed to a one-or-no-car per family pattern while public transportation is making a comeback. The dynamics of such contractions suggest decidedly different content in the schools.

(3) *Excellence versus growth* is another new input for educators to consider. This is an extension of point two. How shall we wean the young from what Toffler

called our throw-away society and begin to restore respect for craftsmanship as distinct from *kitsch* and from mere convenience? How will we begin to teach respect for more durable things?

(4) *Developing a sense of fulfillment based on satisfaction rather than possession.* Really such satisfaction often resides in one's creative achievements with hand or mind. How can the curriculum and instruction, broadly conceived, make these satisfactions more widespread? Perhaps Rebecca West gave as good a clue as any when she wrote:

> . . . a nation should be . . . a shelter where all talents are generously recognized, all forgivable oddities forgiven, all viciousness quietly frustrated, and those who lack talent honored for equivalent contributions of graciousness.

(5) Yet another challenge is to create, at least in part through schooling, *a recycling society.* In the 1970s we reutilize in some form about a third of our bottles, cans, garbage, and dilapidated consumer goods. Our target should first be 90 percent and then as close to 99 percent as we can come. From early childhood, educational experiences in years ahead will need to redevelop the nineteenth-century spirit echoed in the 1920s by Calvin Coolidge when he said, "Use it up, wear it out, and make it do."

(6) *We need to help the young to understand the potential richness of a service-oriented society.* Already, either as producers or consumers of educational services, one-third of the United States goes to school. There are other ways in which a service-and-people centered (rather than thing-centered) culture can be furthered. Better nursing, more paramedical care, better maintained parks and beaches, improved care for young mothers, for the very young, for the aged—all of these require human hands, human minds, and *agapé,* the Greek term connoting love of one's fellows. Human experience is full of the satisfaction of service. Our task, through education, is to enhance recognition for its importance and to restructure an award system that respects service more adequately without downgrading skill and talent.

(7) *Refining the merits of simple communal living* today to match the virtues of pioneer life in a younger America. Although sometimes unfairly stigmatized as peopled by eccentrics and irresponsibles, the contemporary back-to-the-land or simple life movement has much to recommend it for human closeness, the satisfaction of accomplishment through toil, the lack of ostentation, and the cooperative spirit. In our schools, the curriculum might well be modified to enhance the spirit of the closely knit group as it existed in the Jamestown and Plymouth days and on into the twentieth century in rural America. Today, even in the most disadvantaged metrocore, the need for nurturing the communal spirit within individual family groups has sustained itself under the most adverse of circumstances.

(8) *Make more effective use of educational TV, packages, and school-and-home learning techniques.* At a cost of perhaps a penny a day per viewer, TV of a superior sort is one of our neglected educational resources for tomorrow's learners. The trick is to blend curricular and technical know-how with a dash of administrative skill. A most promising idea, if adopted to the U.S. scene is Britain's Open University. A mere gleam of an idea in 1969, the Open University will in a year or two provide access to continuing education for 65,000 learners.

(9) *Recognizing that a measure of mutual coercion will be necessary* for the general welfare if we are to bring off and to enforce the social and educational changes that the future demands. These nine controversial curricular considerations are fraught with potential dissent, a dissent that will be based on fear. But as Gabor noted, "fear is a bad counselor and we must avoid its fatal feedback loop." As Roszak puts it, we can move forward, "a new society piecing itself together inventively within the interstices of the old." But how?

I have previously put on the record my attempt to find an answer:

> It seems reasonable to argue that, in education and in other fields of endeavor, we need new authority structures

that won't dehumanize us but that also will get results. The task is to find a solid middle ground between anarchy and autocracy. To borrow an idea from Garrett Hardin, perhaps we need to work toward a form of participatory democracy in which uncoerced decisions are reached with regard to the mutual coercion that is required to protect us from ourselves. This requires a word of elaboration.

Some of us drive cars that are more of a threat to the environment than need be. An example: the $36,000 Rolls Royce that Stirling Moss road-tested last autumn—a vehicle which he said consumed almost seven [imperial] gallons of gas in one 36-mile stretch of city driving. Or consider any large Detroit product. It requires a great deal of irreplaceable material such as steel or copper and uses three or four times as much of our fossil fuel reserves as would a smaller car. Furthermore, it fouls the air to an alarming extent. Here we need to reach an uncoerced decision as to whether the world needs such extravagant and poisonous transportation. If it doesn't make sense, then we need to engage in "mutual coercion" by passing laws that limit size and gas consumption in our cars, and also begin to restore public transportation to its lost level of usefulness.

In education, too, we need to "coerce ourselves" to do more sensible things with respect to making workable the authority structure that we need. We also need to be sure that the traditions of democracy are respected in the process. But how do we achieve participatory democracy in a culture splintered by pluralism and at the same time *have* someone in control? It is pointless to debate *who* will control the schools if there is no way to *exercise* control.

John Dewey gave us an important lead in resolving this problem when, in 1903, he suggested that leadership should reside in the merit of ideas. Every teacher, he wrote, should have "some regular and representative way in which he or she can register judgment upon matters of educational importance with the assurance that this judgment (if it has merit) will somehow affect the school system. . . ." Today, we would no doubt wish to extend this concept so that the ideas of all—children, parents, administrators, teachers, and so on—can find expression in the educational free market of ideas and, when they pass coinage (i.e., when they have merit), will lead us to the *uncoerced* decisions that will provide a suitable basis for the mutual coercion needed to enforce policies.

Leadership in education must have the power to lead, including the "control" which resides in the power to coerce when enforcing an *uncoerced* group decision. Hegel wrote that freedom is the recognition of necessity." Let us not deceive ourselves: It is a necessity that control of education, with proper restraints, be clearly vested in someone, and we need to retain and to increase *merited* respect for this duly constituted authority. Referenda and recall procedures, clearly established with respect to both *ideas* and *people*, should provide the needed protection against resurgence of a control autocracy, particularly with the independence that teachers have achieved in the past 25 years.

Time should provide many improvements to the ideas expressed here regarding mutual *coercion* based on participatory *democracy*. At the moment, however, this approach to disciplining ourselves for our own best good as we face the controversial implications of futures research impresses me as having more than enough promise to merit study and exploration.

## CONCLUDING STATEMENT

As I look back over the typescript for the PDK monograph, I find there is much that I have failed to communicate with respect to the educationally portentous ideas and suggestions of futures research specialists. The intricate nature of some of their ideas often created a pattern too difficult to portray in a hundred-odd pages.

My exposure to the terrain of futures research also swept away my illusion that I could definitively and succinctly summarize or describe biofutures, sociofutures, and technofutures likely to influence U.S. education. Nonetheless, I hope this report will provide some solid mortar as we continue to redesign and rebuild our schools; that it will help further to extend and to sharpen our imagination and vision and strengthen the will to change many of our practices and procedures. At the very least, I trust that the ideas of futurists will not add to the lyric disorder of some of the critics and commentators who have—with impossible dreams or deft sarcasm—done rather little to help create the solid, acceptable changes that most professional educators have recognized are long overdue.

For me, at least, the futurists' reform agenda for education in tomorrow's world left four indelible impressions:

(1) Through schooling *and* education in their many forms, we should seek to repair the symbiosis that must exist between humankind and nature.

(2) We have perhaps a dozen years—let us say until 1985, one year past Orwell's dismal 1984—to make basic and educationally relevant policy decisions with regard to certain major crises and problems confronting us. Most of these difficulties we must at first face alone because they first became acute in the United States. But the crises potentially are worldwide, and we are irrevocably committed to participate in reforms on a global scale.

(3) Fundamental reforms that feature a new flexibility and humanism are needed in U.S. education. At the same time, in this new context, personalized substantive learning, strong self-discipline, and carefully developed *future-focused* motivation for the learner must be present.

(4) To increase the vigor of our efforts to create better tomorrows, we must stop believing—or pretending—that many of our material comforts are necessities. If we deem them indispensable, then we will mortgage the world to a point at which our children can no longer redeem it.

In his well-known "House Divided" speech, Abraham Lincoln said:

> If we could first know where we are, and whither we are tending, we could then better judge what to do and how to do it.

These twenty-six words, their age not withstanding, are an excellent summary of a simple and fundamental truth that futures research is reestablishing. Surely U.S. education will profit from the study of "whither we are tending" and what to do about it!

## FOOTNOTES

[1]The term "transposed" is used in lieu of "promoted." Presumably one cannot be promoted in an unbroken or seamless curriculum through which he moves without the artificial promotions that now take him from one grade to another.

[2]The concept of "group norms" based on evaluation instruments would disappear. They would be replaced by "personalized norms;" i.e., quantified data on samplings of personal progress data for large groups of individuals sharing certain characteristics as to health, sex, intelligence, and so forth. This does not mean that standards would be abolished but the criteria would be different. That is, two persons of widely different abilities and performance levels might be equally successful if each performed at his full capacity.

[3]It must be borne in mind that grade grouping often subsumes and conceals enormous ability differences in today's schools. The last year in which I taught grade four, spring achievement test profiles for the group ranged from Paul, with a second grade, eighth month score, to Sally who made 8.5! Obviously, continuum-type progress would help to alleviate such unit classroom discrepancies.

[4]Opinions of policy researchers regarding the nature and extent of the preparation of teacher's aides, paramedics, technicians, and the like are varied. Considerable opposition exists to extensive formal preparation lest, by such preparation, various paraprofessionals become specialized to the point that, say, as teacher's aides, they price themselves out of the market by becoming more skilled than need be for services in schools with differentiated staffing.

[5]Some British institutions have a "mature student" category which not only permits but encourages eclectic as well as prescribed studies; a category that might be explored more fully in the U.S.

[6]The residency concept would be especially important during the next decade since some universities are not now preparing teachers to work either in teams or in differentiated teaching partnerships. The residency

should serve to provide the necessary apprenticeship or added preparation that often is needed. At the college and university level, teaching partnerships conceivably could be established to include not only the various academic ranks but mature graduate students in residencies as well. There also should be a role for permanent college and university personnel who have, say, an M.A. plus thirty to sixty hours but who have not completed a doctorate and do not intend to. Their special emphasis would be instruction, and let us note that the Ph.D. and Ed.D. dissertation experience (as now constituted) contribute little or nothing to skillful *classroom* performance.

[7]It must be recognized that the new curricular emphases presented would assume many and different forms with children of varied age levels. With younger learners, a way of ecologically sound living would be based mostly on example and simple precept. In the university phase of the curriculum continuum, however, one might, for example, in a school of architecture or engineering find that *how* to build an airport or a thousand foot building is carefully linked to the study of *whether*, and if so *where*, construction occurs to avoid further damage to the biosphere. Here is an example, too, of cross-disciplinary study that is emerging in heretofore "unrelated" fields such as architecture and biology or biochemistry.

[8]Barry Commoner, *The Closing Circle*. New York: Alfred A. Knopf, 1971, p. 299.

## BIBLIOGRAPHY

Anderson, Robert H., Almy, Millie, Shane, Harold G., and Tyler, Ralph. *Education in Anticipation of Tomorrow.* Worthington, Ohio: Charles A. Jones, 1973.

Andrews, Lewis M. and Karlins, Marvin. *Requeim for Democracy?* New York: Holt, Rinehart and Winston, Inc., 1971, 148pp.

Bassett, T. Robert. "It's the Side Effects of Education That Count", *Phi Delta Kappan.* September, 1972. Pp. 16-17.

Beckwith, Burnham P. *The Next 500 Years.* New York: Beckwith Press, 1967.

Bhagwati, Jagdish N. *Economics and World Order: From the 1970's to the 1990's.* New York: Macmillan, 1973.

Booz, Allen, and Hamilton, Inc. *New Uses and Management Implications of PERT.* New York: Booz, Allen, and Hamilton, Inc., 1964.

Bowers, John, Hoagland, G., Hine, W., and Patterson, Amos. *The Communiversity.* Bloomington, Ind.: The School of Education (Lithographed). 35 pp.

Bright, James R. *A Brief Introduction to Technology Forecasting: Concepts and Exercises.* Permaquid Press, 1972.

Brown, Lester R. *World Without Borders.* New York: Random House, 1972.

Calder, Nigel. *Technopolis: The Social Control of the Uses of Science.* Norwich, England: Fletcher & Son, Ltd. (Panther Books Edition), 1970. 381 pp.

Cellarius, Richard A., and John Platt. "Councils of Urgent Studies," *Science,* 177:670-676, August 25, 1972.

Charter, S.P.R. *The Choice and the Threat.* New York: Ballentine Books, 1972.

Chase, Stuart. *The Most Probable World.* Evanston: Harper and Row, 1968.

Cole, H.S.D., Freeman, Christopher, Jahoda, Marie, Pavitt, K.L.R. (eds.). *Models of Doom: A Critique of the Limits to Growth.* Universe Books, 1973.

Commoner, Barry. *The Closing Circle.* New York: Alfred A. Knopf, Inc., 1971.

Dale, Edgar. "What Can Literature Do?" *The News Letter.* November, 1967.

Dalkey, Norman C. and Rourke, Daniel L., *Experimental Assessment of Delphi Procedures with Group Value Judgments.* Santa Monica, Calif.: RAND Corporation, 1971.

de Brigard, Raul and Helmer, Olaf. *Some Potential Developments-1970-2000.* Middletown, Conn.: Institute for the Future, 1970.

deChardin, Teilhard. *The Phenomenon of Man.* Evanston: Harper & Row, 1955.

deJouvenel, Bertrand. *The Art of Conjecture*. New York: Basic Books, 1967.

De Voto, Bernard. "The Century," *Harper's Magazine*, 201:49-58, October, 1950.

Dickens, Charles. "A Christmas Carol" in Charles H. Sylvester (ed.), *Journeys Through Bookland*. Chicago: Bellows-Reeve Co., 1909. Vol. VII, 138 pp.

Dickson, Paul. *Think Tanks*. New York: Atheneum, 1971.

Dobzhansky, Theodosius. *The Biology of Ultimate Concern*. London: Collins Press, 1971. (The Fontana Library Edition), 152 pp.

Drucker, Peter F. "Saving the  Crusade", *Harper's*, 244:66-71, January, 1972.

Drucker, Peter. *The Age of Discontinuity*. New York: Harper & Row, 1969.

Ehrensvaerd, Goesta. Before—After. (Reviews in the Bloomington, Ind. *Herald-Telephone*, January 11, 1972, p. 18.)

"The Enmity Between Generations", quoted in *The Indianapolis Star*. January 10, 1970.

"The Exploration of the Future," *Réalités*, 245:50-58, June, 1966. (Translated from the French by R. Neiswender for The RAND Collection, P-3540. February, 1967.)

"*Faut-il Stopper La Société de Consommation?*" *Paris Match*, July, 1972. Pp. 40-57.

Feinberg, Gerald. *The Prometheus Project*. New York: Doubleday & Company, Inc., 1969.

Folk, Michael. "Computers and Educational Futures Research" in Michael Marien and Warren L. Ziegler (eds.). *The Potential of Educational Futures*. Worthington, Ohio: Charles A. Jones, 1972. Chapter V.

Forrester, Jay W. *Urban Dynamics*. Cambridge, Mass.: Massachusetts Institute of Technology Press, 1969.

Forrester, Jay W. *World Dynamics*. Wright-Allen Press, 1971.

Friere, Paulo. *Pedagogy of the Oppressed*. New York: Herder & Herder, 1972.

Fuller, Buckminster. "Geoview: Heartbeats and Illions," *World*, 2:44-45, March 13, 1973.

Fuller, Buckminster. "Thinking Out Loud: Disproving the Population Explosion," *World*, July 13, 1973. Pp. 16-40. (Part I of a three-part series.)

Gabor, Dennis. *The Mature Society*. New York: Praeger Publishers, 1972.

Green, Thomas (ed.). *Educational Planning in Perspective*. Guildford, Surrey, England: IPC Science and Technology Press, Limited, 1971.

"The Half Century," *Time*, 55:26-43, January 2, 1950.

Hall, Edward T. *The Hidden Dimension*. Garden City, New York: Doubleday, 1966.

Hall, Edward T. *The Silent Language.* Garden City, New York: Double-day, 1959.

Hardin, Garrett. "The Tragedy of the Commons," *Science,* December 13, 1968, pp. 1243-1248.

Harman, Willis W. *Alternative Futures and Educational Policy.* Menlo Park, Calif.: Stanford Research Institute, 1970.

Helmer, Olaf. *The Future of Science,* in *The Science Journal,* 1967.

Helmer, Olaf. *Social Technology.* New York: Basic Books, 1966.

Hudson Institute Study: *The Corporate Environment 1975-1985.* Croton-on-Hudson, N.Y.: Hudson Institute, 1971.

Jencks, Christopher. *Inequality: A Reassessment of the Effect of Family and Schooling in America.* New York: Basic Books, 1972.

Kahn, Herman. "The Squaring of America," *Intellectual Digest,* 3:16-19. September, 1972.

Kahn, Herman and Briggs, Bruce B. *Things to Come: Thinking About the 70's and 80's.* New York: The Macmillan Company, 1972. 262 pp.

Kahn, Herman and Wiener, Anthony J. *The Year 2000, A Framework for Speculation.* New York: The Macmillan Company, 1967.

Kilpatrick, William H. *Education for a Changing Society.* New York: Macmillan, 1926.

"*Les savants scrutent l'avenir,*" *Réalités,* 237:106-111. Octobre, 1965.

"*Les savants scrutent l'avenir,*" *Réalités,* 236:80-85. Septembre, 1965.

Lessing, Lawrence. "Systems Invades the City," *Fortune.* January, 1968. 157 pp.

Little, Dennis L. and Gordon, Theodore J. *Some Trends Likely to Affect American Society in the Next Several Decades.* Middletown, Conn.: Institute for the Future, 1971.

Longstreet, Wilma. *Beyond Jencks: The Myth of Equal Schooling.* Washington, D.C.: Association for Supervision and Curriculum Development, 1973.

McHale, John. *The Future of the Future.* New York: George Braziller, 1969.

Madden, Carl H. *Clash of Culture: Management in an Age of Changing Values.* National Planning Association, 1972.

Maddox, John. *The Doomsday Syndrome.* New York: McGraw-Hill, 1972.

Marien, Michael. *Alternative Futures for Learning, An Annotated Bibliography.* Syracuse, N.Y.: Educational Policy Research Center, 1971.

Marien, Michael (ed.). *The Hot List Delphi: An Exploratory Survey of Essential Reading for the Future.* Syracuse: University Research Corporation, 1972.

Marien, Michael. *Essential Reading for the Future of Education* (Revised). Syracuse, N.Y.: Educational Policies Research Center, 1971. 71 pp. (Annotated supplement to the original Marian bibliography.)

Marien, Michael and Ziegler, Warren Z. (eds.). *The Potential of Educational Futures.* The NSSE Series, "Contemporary Educational Issues." Worthington, Ohio: Charles A. Jones Publishing Company, 1972.

Meadows, D. H., et al. *The Limits to Growth.* London: Earth Island, Ltd., 1972. 205 pp.

Medawar, Sir Peter. *The Hope of Progress.* London: Methuen and Co. Ltd., 1972.

Meeker, Robert J. and Weiler, Daniel M. *A New School for the Cities.* Santa Monica, Calif.: System Development Corporation, 1970.

Michael, Donald N. "*L'avenir du Temps Libre,*" *Economie et humanisme,* 167:3-12, Mai/Juin, 1966.

Michael, Donald N. *The Unprepared Society: Planning for a Precarious Future.* New York: Basic Books, 1968.

Moon, Rexford G., Jr. *National Planning for Education.* New York: Academy for Educational Development, Inc., 1970.

Muller, Herbert J. *The Children of Frankenstein.* Bloomington, Ind.: Indiana University Press, 1970.

Olson, Paul A., Freeman, Larry, Bowman, James (eds.). *Education for 1984 and After.* Lincoln, Neb.: Study Commission on Undergraduate Education and the Education of Teachers, 1971.

Perisco, Connell F. and McEachron, Norman B. *Forces for Societal Transportation in the United States, 1950-2000.* Menlo Park, Calif.: Stanford Research Institute, 1971.

Platt, John. "A Fearful and Wonderful World for Living," Mimeographed, 21 pp. Paper presented at the Home Economics Centennial Symposium, Families of the Future; Ames, Iowa, October 5, 1971.

Platt, John. "Science for Human Survival," *The Science Teacher,* 40:1, January, 1973.

Platt, John. "How Men Can Shape Their Futures," *Futures,* 3:32-47, March, 1971.

Platt, John. "What We Must Do," *Science,* 166:1115-1121, November 28, 1969.

Reich, Charles A. *The Greening of America.* New York: Bantam, 1971.

Revel, Jean-François. *Without Marx or Jesus.* Garden City, N.Y.: 1971.

Rosenfeld, Stephen S. "Robert S. McNamara and the Wiser Use of Power," *World,* July 13, 1973, Pp. 18-24.

Roszak, Theodore. *Where the Wasteland Ends.* New York: Doubleday and Company, 1972.

Shane, Harold G. "Future Shock and the Curriculum," *Phi Delta Kappan,* 49:67-70, October, 1967.

Shane, Harold G. "Looking to the Future: Reassessment of Educational

Issues of the 1970's," *Phi Delta Kappan*, 54:326-337, January, 1973.

Shane, Harold G. "Prospects and Prerequisites for the Improvement of Elementary Education," Chapter XV in *The Elementary School in the United States*. 72nd Yearbook of the NSSE, Part II. Chicago: University of Chicago Press, 1973.

Shane, Harold G. "The Rediscovery of Purpose in Education," *Educational Leadership*, 28:581-584, March, 1971.

Shane, Harold G. "The Educational Significance of the Future" Mimeographed. A special report to the U.S. Commissioner of Education, 1972.

Shane, June Grant, *et al. Guiding Human Development*. Worthington, Ohio: Charles A. Jones Publishing Co., 1971.

"Slowdown on Research," *Time Magazine*, July 2, 1973, p. 46.

"Split Views on America," *Time Magazine*, December 25, 1972. European Edition, p. 20.

Taylor, Gordon R. *The Doomsday Book: Can The World Survive?* New York: World Book Company, 1972. 366pp.

Theobald, Robert. *Futures Conditional*. Indianapolis: Bobbs-Merrill Company, Inc., 1971. 359pp.

Thompson, William I. *At the Edge of History*. Evanston: Harper Colophon, 1971.

Toffler, Alvin. "The Future as a Way of Life," *Horizons*. Summer, 1965.

Toffler, Alvin. *Future Shock*. New York: Random House, 1970.

Toffler, Alvin, *et al., Learning for Tomorrow*. New York: Random House, 1974.

"Toward a National Materials Policy," *World*, May 22, 1973.

Wagar, W. Warren. *Building the City of Man*. New York: Grossman, 1971.

Wallia, C. S. (ed.). *Toward Century 21*. New York: Basic Books, Inc., 1970.

Ward, Barbara and Dubos, Réné. *Only One Earth: The Care and Maintenance of a Small Planet*. New York: W. W. Norton and Company, Inc., 1972. 225 pp.

Ways, Max. "The Road to 1977," *Fortune*, January, 1967.

**APPENDIX:**
**RECOMMENDATIONS TO THE U.S. COMMISSIONER**
**OF EDUCATION EXCERPTED FROM THE ORIGINAL**
**USOE REPORT, "THE EDUCATIONAL SIGNIFICANCE**
**OF THE FUTURE."** Contract No. OEC-0-72-0354

## APPENDIX:
## RECOMMENDATIONS TO THE U.S.
## COMMISSIONER OF EDUCATION

During the six months since *The Educational Significance of the Future* first was circulated among government employees, congressmen, and the futures research personnel who participated in the original survey, there have been a number of requests for the 34-page precis and for the 135-page original.[1]

While this PDK monograph is an elaboration of most of the full report, it does not include in the body of the text the thirty-four recommendations presented during the autumn of 1972 to Sidney P. Marland, Jr., then commissioner of education and presently assistant secretary of Health, Education, and Welfare.

The recommendations, with a few editorial changes to increase their clarity, are presented on the following pages:

1. Broad focal points for the USOE: tactics and strategies suggested by future research, pp. 103 to 107.
2. Recommendations: specific suggestions for research and development in education between 1973 and 1985, pp. 107 to 111.
3. Proposals aimed at the elementary and secondary school levels, pp. 111 to 113.
4. Post-secondary education, pp. 113 to 115.

---

[1]The original document, compressed into 73 pages, is available for $3.00 from The World Future Society, Box 30369, Bethesda Station, Washington, D.C. 20014.

## CONCLUSIONS AND RECOMMENDATIONS

The educational significance of the future resides in four propositions. *First,* we can choose rationally among alternative futures, *ceteris paribus,* and in the process of doing so we can also begin to fulfill our social prophecies with respect to the quality of life we want to achieve. *Second,* we have an opportunity to create a continuum of lifelong education opportunities of such patent value that the public's wavering moral and financial support for the schools can be restored and increased. *Third,* a continuum of lifelong learning can be conceived of as teaching and learning which transcends our present systems of schooling; teaching and learning with many problems gone and only virtue remaining in new instructional environments. *Fourth,* we already have many excellent and important resources and potential innovations in the U.S. educational idea bin. By refining and using them during the next decade, a unique approach to equitable education can be made within the present basic structure of the educational community.

1. **Broad focal points for the USOE: tactics and strategies suggested by futures research.** The four chapters that follow provide the substance of this report. However, without the present summary they are like a mosaic, one for which the design is ready and for which the stones have been cut, but which has not been pieced together to provide a panorama of the educational terrain of the next five to fifteen years. Although the following "educational tactics and strategies" draw on the material presented in detail in later chapters, they are more than a summary. They serve as a guide book giving suggestions regarding a suitable route across the educational terrain which is covered in Chapter II through V [of the original report].

The recommendations for research and development have been numbered for the reader's convenience and to help identify main routes to follow in the quest for a desirable reformation in U.S. education.

(1.1) *Seamless curriculum.* The most important single strategy for the USOE to employ in the next decade is one of moving toward a seamless, lifetime continuum of educational opportunity. Chapter IV contains (a) the rationale for this move, (b) a description, with models, of the structure of such a continuum, and (c) an explanation of the teaching partnerships which supersede team teaching in a continuum. (See figs. 6, 7, and 8.)

(1.2) *Idea gap.* An important strategy in future development is to narrow and, if possible, to close the "Idea Gap" that exists between the USOE and some U.S. educators. Patently, the mission of the USOE is limited by statute and restrictions as to funding. Nevertheless, it exerts powerful influence which probably will increase as its service and research functions grow in the coming decade. Therefore, state and local personnel need to know more rapidly and completely what is developing with respect to educational renewal and reform, what state and local personnel can and can't do, and what goals federal leadership seeks as the USOE works to advance the national interest. It is easy to propose that the idea gap be closed; quite another matter to remedy the problem. For one thing, Regional Offices of the USOE might be urged to study coping tactics. More deliberate planning of briefing sessions for state school officers and key superintendents and deans is needed. These briefings could be held early at such meetings as those of the AACTE, AASA, AERA, or ASCD. But most important—according to survey data—is the reduction of the "crisis-and-crash-program" approach to multimillion dollar spending by preliminary study, exploratory discussion, and long-term study designs.

(1.3) *Avoid overemphasis on the atypical and culturally different.* A third important strategy is to deploy funding and energy at *all* levels of education rather than merely to place greatest emphasis on the poor, the culturally different, *et cetera.* Freud's contributions would have been even more broad and deep if he had not concentrated so extensively on troubled or disturbed patients. The USOE in the coming decade should not repeat the "Freudian error" of working too exclusively with atypical children and youth and with problem situations to the neglect of the larger pupil population.

(1.4) *Change strategies.* For the next several years more emphasis should be placed on change *strategies* and proportionately less time on *innovations.* We already know some directions in which to go, ergo the USOE should stress the *how*-to-proceed tactics that will move us forward. This should help to alleviate the very real problem that resides in the lack of implementation of *yesterday's* innovations.

(1.5) *Student involvement in program planning.* More stress should be placed on the importance of mature students being involved in and responsible for planning *their own* programs. We also should endeavor to reduce academic red tape at the secondary and post-secondary levels. While encouraging freedom to plan, we should emphasize the consequences of students' faulty choices.

(1.6) *Alternative forms of education.* We should continue to support alternative forms of education—particularly those involving responsible community participation—but with especial emphasis on research on projects which promise results without greatly increasing the per capita cost of instruction. The concept of the *paracurriculum* (cf. Chap. IV) is particularly important in this connection as is the proposed new concept of seamless post-secondary education.

(1.7) *Career choice strategies.* Through mass media and the strategic deployment of funds, we should try to encourage non-collegebound youth to make realistic, satisfying career choices—insofar as possible—in technical, service, and production type jobs. Also we should consider selective funding of post-secondary students to encourage their entry into fields where manpower needs seem most likely to exist.

(1.8) *Financing post-secondary education.* In the face of

increasing resistance to the rising cost of education, we should explore new ways of supporting higher education so that the beneficiaries of this education pay a larger share of the cost. It is recognized that current legislation has a bearing on this point. Nonetheless, it is suggested that the federal government consider financing post-secondary students by further study of such devices as interest-free loans to students rather than paying for education entirely or largely from conventional revenue resources. Loans up to $20,000 might for instance, become interest-bearing upon graduation. They also might be counted as tax-deductible in each of the years in which they were repaid in annual installments in an amount of the student's own choosing. To insure repayment if the loans are not repaid five years after graduation, modest interest and principal payments could be added in proportion to the debtor's earnings when he reported his income to the Internal Revenue Service.

(1.9) *Future-oriented teacher preparation.* Since most undergraduates in education probably are being prepared for schools as they are today, it would be prudent to begin now to study tactics for the education of future-oriented teachers for 1980s classrooms. Their experiences should sensitize them to alternative social, biological, and technological futures and problems, include new content and recent developments in methods, involve them in new approaches to (or substitutes for) student teaching, emphasize personal strategies for coping with information overload in their academic specialties, help them grasp what their roles are in a lifelong educational continuum, and emphasize preparation for work in situations involving differentiated staffing.

(1.10) *Shared responsibility for teacher preparation.* As a corollary of point nine above, encourage close cooperation between local communities and teachers colleges in preservice and inservice education ventures. The model in Figure 8 in Chapter IV deals with staff deployment. It includes the idea of having young teachers in *residency* during their first year of service and jointly supervised and guided by both school district and teacher education institution.

(1.11) *Accountability.* Begin to interpret "accountability" in three dimensions: (a) community, (b) school, and (c) child. About 100 years ago the U.S. *community* of Tom Sawyer's day probably was more accountable than it is today. The testing movement, *circa* 1930 made the *child* accountable, while in the 1960s the *schools* were pressured to become accountable. Balance among the accountability responsibilities of all three needs to be restored. An important research study might deal with the meaning and nature of "balanced accountability" in education as well as with how to achieve it on a broader basis than on performance *per se.*

(1.12) *"New impact" research in substantive fields.* We should endeavor to encourage, in all disciplines, new impact research with a bearing on education. We seem since the late 1960s to be in a valley between crests of seminal research and its applications. Fresh and novel research should recognize and, if possible, help to reconcile the three-way split among the proponents of didactic (telling), heuristic (discovery), and humanistic (self-actualizing) approaches to instruction. More explicitly, federal agencies such as the National Institute of Education might seek to stimulate a "second round" of research in disciplines related to education (and involving professional educators) analagous to those that led to the "new math" of a decade or more ago.

2. **Recommendations: specific suggestions for research and development in education between 1973 and 1985.** The proposals below tend to maximize the importance of long-range (ten to fifteen years) planning versus the advantages of short-term (two to three years) plans conducted under USOE and/or NIE auspices. They also emphasize, when possible, the importance of participation and of process in planning—but take careful note of the need to create and

to maintain situations which permit strong leadership to function.

*General Proposals.* A number of the recommendations are intended to stress the need to clarify our educational goals in a time of uncertainty and value-crisis, and to shift more of our efforts from quantitative and materialistic to criteria for "good" education to greater heed for quality-of-life (QOL) factors in both schooling and the totality of educational experience.

It should be kept in mind that the proposals below are based on intensive interviews with futurists. Different or additional suggestions might have come from other sources. The recommendations follow:

(2.1) *Implementing a lifelong learning continuum.* It is suggested that an experimental seamless curriculum continuum be developed in one of the "New Cities" such as the Minnesota Experimental City or under the aegis of the Experimental Schools programs that recently have been funded. Patently, the idea of implementing a seamless learning continuum can only be done by a large educational unit such as, say, Minneapolis or in a major New Cities setting. As noted in Chapter IV, the continuum would extend from early childhood education through old age and, if possible, should include community college or "communiversity" resources for many years of non-terminal and highly diversified post-secondary education predominantly if not exclusively on a non-credit basis. In the writer's opinion, this may prove to be the single most important recommendation made in the report. Furthermore, it could be of an educational interest and significance that transcends such historic ventures as the Eight Year Study (1934-1942).

(2.2) *Penetration of the education field by business.* We should sponsor a study, or perhaps a continuing center, to explore the flow of new developments in the "Business-in-Education" field. The penetration of education by business may well suggest important new cooperative relationships among the school, government agencies, and U.S.

business. What, for example, can be done to explore and profit educationally from the importance of a multibillion dollar corporation building and operating schools for a large city independent of the community's established school system?

(2.3) *Futures research conferences.* Consider having the two USOE Educational Policy Research Centers jointly sponsor in the Washington area a three-phase futures planning conference. It would be valuable for such meetings (a) to identify biological, sociological, and technological developments with a direct bearing on human futures and on education, (b) to study their social consequences, and (c) to advise the commissioner with respect to an action agenda for the USOE. Questions pertaining to values, to equity in education, and to realistic goals for schooling should be given priority in such a futures research investment. Also, considerable attention should be given to the implications of biochemical research related to learning and to developments in electrical stimulation of the brain in view of futurists' opinions regarding the importance of such research.

(2.4) *Careers and social needs research.* A vocationally-oriented study should be undertaken to ascertain the extent to which older children and youth have occupational aspirations that are congruent with governmental data and social indicators with a bearing on prospects for their employment, social need, and educational plans. Data obtained could be used to guide schools and vocational or career guidance personnel in helping the young develop a suitable future-focused role image.

(2.5) *Research data and input for developing educational media.* Teaching aids of all sorts are powerful determinants of what is taught in U.S. schools. It is recommended therefore, that an exploratory study be made in at least one of the four major areas of academic concentration in U.S. schools (language arts, science, mathematics, social studies) to determine whether there is as yet a central tendency as to agreement in curriculum content after fifteen years of curriculum reform. If such a tendency exists, it is urged that a broad overview of content and an inventory of needed teaching aids, in a given field be prepared and outlined in detail. This is not a proposal for a "national curriculum." Rather it is an attempt to identify a desirable body of content, *with suggested supportive aids,* and with decisions as to the scope, sequence, and pacing of instruction left to the professional judgment of individual teachers or teams in the local school unit. The results of such a study or studies should be invaluable to curriculum workers, stimulate activity in education-related disciplines, and provide ideas and guidelines for instructional systems, technology personnel, and for commercial publishers. Professional associations for teachers and supervisors would welcome involvement and could help to encourage the grass roots penetration of both ideas and media development.

(2.6) *Social indicator inventory.* Behavioral scientists often speak highly of social indicators. It is possible that there would be value in a reverse or hindsight study of socio-educational indicators during the years 1950-1972. Such an inquiry would endeavor to identify subtle factors that were ignored or unrecognized when they might have served as an "early warning system." Data here should be helpful to the extent that indicators of *future* problem situations can be found in the records of the past.

(2.7) *Computerized data bank for students.* An inquiry might be made as to the feasibility of a computerized national data bank for U.S. students. This presumably would contain key academic records of the sort kept in schools' cumulative record folders, but with due respect for the "confidentiality" which many guidance specialists defend. The uniformity, speed of transfer, and widespread availability of data from such a bank recommend that the idea be explored on a pilot basis. A university with suitable resources and adequate support might well serve the entire American educational community.

(2.8) *Future-focused and realistic career guidance.*

Rapid increases in college enrollments, and social indicators such as employment trends, bring to mind the merit of research in secondary school advisement policies and in university admissions policies to fields of study in the context of jobs likely to be available in the late 1970s and 1980s.

(2.9) *Low-cost research through graduate school channels.* The USOE may be overlooking an important freshet of productive low-cost research accomplished through the subsidization of doctoral students seeking thesis topics. It is recommended on an experimental basis that the NIE consider inviting professors in ten universities to apply for small grants (say, $12,000 each for one year). The professors would then recruit and guide ten doctoral students through small-scale research projects chosen from an annotated list prepared by the USOE. An equitable portion of the $12,000 (perhaps 10%) could be utilized by the professor for expenses involved in his personal guidance of the research; the remainder would subsidize the student-scholar.

3. **Proposals aimed at the elementary and secondary school levels.** As a result of conversations with specialists in policies studies, six ventures including research projects are recommended.

(3.1) *Controlled study of lower school-leaving ages.* A carefully controlled and directed study might be made of procedures that might be followed in lowering of the various school-leaving ages now mandated by state law. In a seamless, lifelong educational continuum—one with infinite, planned exit and re-entry privileges—at least some young learners might leave the classroom at from thirteen-fourteen to fifteen-sixteen years of age. Parents, counselors, employers, and other school personnel would need to be involved in a close, sound planning relationship to avoid the danger of exploiting youth. Also, the initial experiment with lower leaving ages would work best in an "open" school continuum such as is described in Chapter IV, and in a setting such as the "New Experimental City" in Minnesota (see point 2.1 above).

(3.2) *Definitive study of the value of early childhood education.* As was noted in the 1972 Yearbook of the NSSE, there is little hard data to lend categorical support to the assumption that early childhood education (ECE) can and will influence the behavior and development of young learners. Since a number of futurists tacitly or explicitly forecast extension of public education downward to age three or four, an eight-year study of children from ages two through nine seems highly important and is recommended. Experimental and control groups of black and white children from diverse social backgrounds should be involved over the eight-year span. The target would be collection of hard data on the comparative social and academic performance of matched nine-year-olds who had and who had not had three years of pre-primary developmental in-school experience.

(3.3) *Realistic cost estimates.* Most suggestions for improving education in the future seem to involve further substantial financial outlays. It is urged that any programs of a massive or extensive nature be projected by the NIE and USOE contracting parties to ascertain their costs at annual or biennial intervals if instituted on a wide scale. A case in point: it has been estimated by one futurist that if all of the objectives in *Goals for Americans* (1960 Report of the President's Commission on National Goals) had been achieved the annual cost would have been three times the yearly GNP of the United States during that era.

(3.4) *Financial strain in school districts.* Research might be conducted in one or more of our twenty largest cities to ascertain whether (and, if so, when) present trends in elementary and secondary programs could lead to school unit bankruptcy. A study of viable preventive measures should be included.

(3.5) *Research in the realm of legal rights and responsibilities.* A major legal study probably is needed to ascertain what constraints and what open avenues there are for innovations and alternative schools, compulsory attendance, student-teacher-parent rights and responsibilities, flexible accreditation and admissions, tuition charges, and diversified staffing.

(3.6) *Diversified staff deployment.* There needs to be greater study of the nature and of the merits of diversified staffing including the teaching partnership concept presented in Chapter IV. Diversified staffing should be the object of examination at all levels (also cf. 4.3 below).

4. **Post-secondary education.** Imaginative and "open" approaches to innovations and to economies at the post-secondary school level are needed. Rapid growth in enrollments since World War II, and especially since 1960, has created certain imbalances and academic traditions more reminiscent of cottage industry than of mass production.

(4.1) *Education for learners past sixty.* The concept of lifelong educational opportunity extending to age seventy or beyond needs to be contemplated. Should there, for instance, be provisions for "old married" housing on the 1985 campus? At present one of the great unexplored educational regions is that of the fifty-five to eighty-plus learner. Studies in this area need to involve both policy (admission, credit, tuition, etc.) and program (content, goals, individualization, new courses, course reorganization, etc.). It seems highly desirable to set a USOE task force to work exploring the alternative futures for senior learners as well as the possible linkages of such futures to an educational continuum, the communiversity concept, and contemporary post-secondary resources for educating the growing above-sixty segment of the population.

(4.2) *Pilot programs for the elderly.* Since the nature of schooling of broader focus of education for the middle-aged and the elderly will be of growing importance, in addition to a task force study, selected secondary schools, communiversities, and major universities should be urged by the USOE to propose pilot programs in the forty to seventy age range to increase our knowledge of potential demand, human needs to be met, and possible costs.

(4.3) *New approaches to student teaching.* An action research venture into a three-year teacher education program (cooperatively designed by community and university) in which student teaching is totally abolished and replaced by a paid, supervised residency should be funded. Much conventional student teaching is not only costly but fails fully to accomplish its purpose. New ways of approaching the development of classroom strategies need to transcend both past practice and the inadequacies of most performance-based criteria ventures explored in the early 1970s.

(4.4) *Better preparation for paraprofessionals.* An analagous program for the carefully planned preparation of teacher aides and of paraprofessionals, both at the secondary and the communiversity level should be encouraged. Presumably, such programs would be for one and two years, respectively, but also would facilitate re-entry to the educational continuum for personnel who demonstrate ability. One important caveat: the preparation of paraprofessionals should not be so extensive as to create substandard *teachers* rather than competent *helpers.*

(4.5) *Differentiated staffing in higher education.* In the interest of economy, and conceivably—at the undergraduate level—of efficiency, there should be consideration of a one- or two-year control group experiment in which conventional instruction competes with lower cost, differentiated staff structures using fewer doctorates. Student achievement, compared in terms of performance criteria established for a substantive field could serve as a basis for evaluation.

(4.6) *De-emphasis of the trend toward a universal Bachelor's degree.* A reeducation program for students, teachers, and parents might well be launched to reverse the century-old practice of advocating the importance of a college education for anyone who can leap the academic, social, and financial hurdles. For years now—at least for two decades—the educational profession and parents have shown too little awareness that a conventional, universal four-year college education *as it is now constituted* may not be inherently desirable for many—perhaps a majority—of young Americans. Continuous methodically planned adult education of comparable quality, greater variety, and increased flexibility is needed as a parallel to the formal higher educational requirements of a credential-permeated society.

(4.7) *Postponement of college admission.* Consider encouraging delayed college admission. There may be distinct value in supporting the idea that students will perform better and will sometimes even permanently bypass costly college attendance (which may be of no practical personal or social utility) if there is a two- to four-year-interval of work experience in which to begin a vocational career. This suggestion is based on two premises, namely, (a) that in an educational continuum adult (non-credit) programs will provide most post-secondary needs beyond the community college level, and (b) that the baccalaureate program as now organized in most colleges is not designed to meet the vocational and social needs of youth on a universalized basis.

This précis of possible educational futures of significance is already overlong. Although several more points should be made particularly with regard to a model for local school unit organization, teacher licensing based on performance, degree-renewal for teachers, it seems clear that a summary should not threaten to exceed the length of the research report!

## LE MALADE IMAGINAIRE?

After a month of intensive discussion interviews with futurists it seems safe to say that education, *unlike* the main character in Moliere's 17th Century play, is not an imaginary invalid. The schools actually *have* been weakened by serious ills just as society has been beset by dangerous crises. At the same time much of the educational significance of the future—as is implicit throughout the report—resides in the fact that the problems are not fatal ones.

We already have in our idea bins some of the basic "frontier ideas" needed to carry us through the 1970s. It therefore becomes the task of leadership at the federal level to strive further to abate the confusion of the waning crises of transition and to build the best of alternative futures on the basis of continued research and development as sketched in the recommendations above.

Emerging opportunities for educational leadership in the USOE and in the NIE make this report on the significance of the future of education even more portentous than it would have been a year ago. Much thought and effort has gone into the development of an infrastructure that promises to facilitate not only research but implementation. With open minds, continued effort, and a measure of luck, USOE-NIE resources should go a long way toward healing the non-fatal illnesses of U.S. schools through heavy doses of implementation—*by making changes that we already have enough knowledge to bring into being.*

Harold G. Shane
Indiana University